Threat to Development: Pitfalls of the NIEO

Also of Interest

† Available in hardcover and paperback.

Westview Special Studies in Social, Political, and Economic Development

Threat to Development: Pitfalls of the NIEO
William Loehr and John P. Powelson

Far from transferring resources from the rich to the poor, as intended, the New International Economic Order (NIEO)—if fully implemented—is more likely to transfer them from the poor to the rich. Thus assert the authors, who present their analysis of trade and investment data in support of their conclusions. The NIEO, a program adopted by the United Nations, proposes increased prices of primary products, tariff preferences for exports of less developed countries to the industrial world, a code of conduct for multinational corporations, international monetary reform, debt forgiveness or rescheduling for the third world, plus a number of other provisions designed to help third-world countries.

But, the authors contend, all these provisions will further enrich the already rich within the third world, while adding to the poverty of the already poor. Higher prices for primary products would benefit the rich producers at the expense of the poor who buy them. Debt rescheduling would help only those rich enough to incur debt in the first place; because aid is available in finite quantities, this help might be at the expense of the poor. Likewise, trade preferences would also help the rich, who are the major exporters.

The NIEO has been widely acclaimed in industrialized as well as in third world countries; this book demonstrates how the effects of the NIEO could well be the opposite from what is widely believed.

William Loehr is an associate professor of economics at the University of Denver. In 1979 he was a visiting professor at the University of Chile. His publications include *The Economics of Development and Distribution* (1981; with J. P. Powelson) and *Public Goods and Public Policy* (1978; edited with Todd Sandler). **John P. Powelson** is a professor of economics at the University of Colorado, Boulder. He has been senior economic adviser to the ministries of finance of Kenya and Bolivia and has published numerous books and papers, including *A Select Bibliography on Economic Development: With Annotations* (Westview, 1979).

Threat to Development: Pitfalls of the NIEO

William Loehr and
John P. Powelson

Westview Press / Boulder, Colorado

Westview Special Studies in Social, Political, and Economic Development

Copyright © 1983 by Westview Press, Inc.

Published in 1983 in the United States of America by
  Westview Press, Inc.
  5500 Central Avenue
  Boulder, Colorado 80301
  Frederick A. Praeger, President and Publisher

Library of Congress Cataloging in Publication Data
Loehr, William.
  Threat to development.
  (Westview special studies in social, political, and economic development)
  Bibliography: p.
  Includes index.
  1. International economic relations. 2. Underdeveloped areas. I. Powelson, John P.,
1920–   II. Title. III. Series.
HF1411.L554   337   82-4777
ISBN 0-86531-128-5   AACR2
ISBN 0-86531-129-3 (pbk.)

Printed and bound in the United States of America

Contents

Figures and Tables

Preface

Since the Declaration of a New International Economic Order (NIEO) was adopted by the United Nations in 1974, its supporters have multiplied. They include not only diplomats from less developed countries (LDCs), but also agencies of the United Nations such as UNCTAD (United Nations Conference on Trade and Development), UNIDO (United Nations Industrial Development Organization), and UNITAR (United Nations Institute for Training and Research). UNITAR has developed a library that includes fifty-seven volumes of material on NIEO. In addition, a support movement has swelled among nongovernmental organizations in more developed countries (MDCs).

These supporters stress that the "old" economic order—the way in which international business and banking have been done—has primarily benefited the rich countries. Relative richness and poverty have been explained, at least in part, by the workings of this old order. We accept this proposition, and it is not what this book is about.

Rather, we believe that a more sober analysis of the proposed "new" order is timely. UN publications refer to the NIEO as a wave of the future, inevitable, and a natural extension of the struggle against colonialism. Perhaps it is, in part. But the declaration is also a document prepared by the governments of less developed countries, and it is not always clear that NIEO represents the interests of the whole country as opposed to the modern-sector elites.

For the most part, we believe that the NIEO is a way of transferring resources from the poor to the rich. The fact that it may do so and still gain wide political support stems from one of the quirks of economic reasoning: The ultimate impact of a proposition may be the opposite of what appears on the surface. We plan to show, in the present book, how that quirk is the case with the principal planks of the NIEO plan and how this fact will ultimately reduce the prospects for its widespread acceptance.

This book can be read by nontechnical as well as technical readers. Generally, little prior knowledge of economics is required. In the instances where an understanding of complex economics principles is important, however, we have attempted to provide illustrative material that will make our points clear to the general reader.

In several places we refer to specific sections or paragraphs of the New International Economic Order. The source of these statements is the *Declaration of the Establishment of a New International Economic Order,* UN Resolution 3201 (S-VI), May 1, 1974 (New York).

W. L.
J.P.P.

Overview

A New Order for Justice?

Economists and diplomats from the third world have long insisted that the conduct of international trade and finance is biased in favor of rich countries. They argue that multinational corporations, banks, and international institutions, aided and abetted by tariffs and other forms of government protection, carry on their business in ways that divert the world's resources, income, and economic development disproportionately to the rich. For at least three decades, these advocates proposed marginal changes or new institutions here and there. Early in the seventies, they began to codify their proposals. The resulting declaration was deemed sufficiently comprehensive, radical, and systemic to be called a New International Economic Order (NIEO). It was passed without vote in the General Assembly of the United Nations on May 1, 1974.

Passage by the General Assembly, however, was only a beginning. The ten articles, with their eighty-five subdivisions, only suggest directions of change; specific results wait upon piecemeal negotiations. Those negotiations have been taking place, but the bulk of the NIEO has not yet been specified, much less agreed upon.

The acclaim for NIEO has not been confined to the third world. It has been echoed by intellectuals, religious organizations, and other people in the more developed countries (MDCs) who profess sympathy toward alleviating the plight of the poor (see Brandt Commission 1980). A great deal of the literature and appeals to their own governments have welled up from these groups.

We share the sympathies of these groups, for our concern also lies with the poor. It lies not just in providing temporary relief, but in shaping a world in which the poor may achieve the knowledge and power to defend themselves politically and economically and to provide for themselves materially. We believe many institutions are biased against

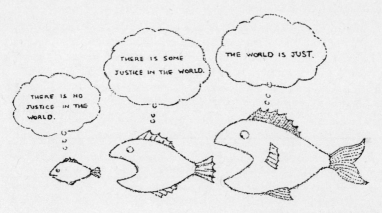

Drawing by Mankoff; © 1981
The New Yorker Magazine, Inc.

FIGURE 1.1

them and that those institutions must be identified and changed. But we believe that, in general, the people who drew up the NIEO selected the wrong institutions and overlooked the real biases. By and large, NIEO was constructed by government officials of the third world, and they did not necessarily represent the poorest of the poor countries or even the poorest within their own countries. If fully implemented, we believe the NIEO would retard the development of the third world and further impoverish its poor.

The core provisions of the NIEO plan are summarized as follows.

First, the prices of exports from less developed countries (LDCs) should be supported in world markets. It is widely believed that the prices of primary-product exports of LDCs do not rise as much, over time, as the prices of manufactured exports from MDCs. Therefore, LDCs pay more and more coffee (tin, cocoa, copper, etc.) for the same number of automobiles (machines, etc.). Together, these relative changes are known as the "terms of trade." To overcome declining terms of trade, NIEO suggests that the prices of LDC exports should be linked to those of MDC exports. LDC diplomats have been negotiating for an international commodity fund that might buy surplus primary products to support their prices.

Second, LDCs should be exempt from customs duties and other import restrictions of MDCs, without the same privilege being extended to other MDCs through most-favored-nation agreements. This practice would be known as the Generalized System of Preferences (GSP).

Third, an international code of conduct could prevent multinational corporations (MNCs) from interfering in the internal affairs of host countries. Technology should be offered more liberally by MDCs to LDCs. Many people have contended that technology flows primarily through MNCs, which either restrict its use to their own subsidiaries or else demand heavy royalty payments.

Fourth, LDCs should have a greater voice in designing rules for the international monetary system (IMS). The IMS consists of all rules and institutions (including banks) by and through which international finance is transacted, and it focuses on the International Monetary Fund (IMF). Among other things, the IMF issues a kind of currency, known as Special Drawing Rights (SDRs), which, with some limitations, can be used to settle international transactions. Currently, new SDRs are distributed roughly in proportion to current holdings of international reserves, thus favoring MDCs. Third world countries would prefer that new SDRs be allocated disproportionately to them to help promote LDC development.

Fifth, debts of LDC governments to MDC governments and banks should be canceled, reduced, or rescheduled.

Sixth, special attention should be paid to food production, so that the world's poor need never go hungry.

Seventh, more financial aid should be provided by MDCs to LDCs, and the latter should have a greater voice in how that aid is used.

Eighth, there should be a greater flow of financial investment from MDCs to LDCs, with greater LDC government control over how the investments will be deployed.

Ninth, the share of LDCs in industrial production should be increased.

The United Nations and the NIEO

Strong support for the NIEO has emerged within the three United Nations agencies mentioned in the Preface (UNCTAD, UNIDO, and UNITAR). In its inaugural meeting in Geneva in 1964, UNCTAD made the following declaration:

> At the root of the foreign trade difficulties facing the developing countries and other countries highly dependent on a narrow range of primary commodities are the slow rate of growth of demand for their exports of primary commodities, accounting for 90 per cent of their exports, the increasing participation of developed countries in world trade in primary commodities, and the deterioration in the terms of trade of developing countries from 1950 to 1962. {UNCTAD 1 1964, p. 8}

From that point on, diplomats of LDCs have tirelessly attempted, through UNCTAD (and more recently, the North-South dialogues), to gain international intervention for improved prices for their raw material exports to MDCs. Indeed, the program set forth in the final act of UNCTAD 1 (1964, p. 9) was virtually copied ten years later in the Program of Action for the NIEO. That document mentioned the need for higher growth rates in LDCs, new guidelines for financial and technical cooperation and aid terms, ways to solve external debt problems, increased financial flows from MDCs to LDCs, and compensatory finance for price fluctuations of commodities, as well as other needs.

Let us look at the question of higher prices for primary products. A key element of NIEO is that higher prices should be paid for primary products (agricultural and mineral). A key supposition is that primary products are produced by poor countries and consumed in rich countries; therefore, higher prices would cause the rich to share resources with the poor. But if the world is divided not into rich and poor countries, but into rich and poor *people*, then one quickly grasps that primary products are largely produced by the rich and largely consumed by the poor. (Although rich and poor both consume primary products, the poor pay a greater proportion of their income for them than the rich.) Therefore, higher prices of primary products would cause a transfer of resources from the poor to the rich, not the other way around.

Summary of the Book

The NIEO declaration contains some proposals we agree with—a world food plan, for example. But, as we expect to show in this book, every one of the key propositions has some kind of "catch" that makes the result of the proposal the opposite of what it appears to be on the surface. It is these "catches" that we plan to explain.

In Chapters 2 through 6, we take up, successively, the principal points of NIEO and explain the "catches" that turn each proposition upside down. What appears on surface as a transfer from rich to poor, in practice would work the other way. In Chapter 7, we bring many of the pieces together, showing how events concerning the price of oil, the world debt situation, and the international monetary system have come together to affect the position of the poor. In Chapter 8, we assess some of the other aspects of NIEO, including some portions of it that we favor. Finally, in Chapter 9, we turn to the internal gap, and we hope to show that a different approach (not NIEO) to the international system would improve conditions for the poor of the LDCs.

In the following sections of this chapter, we present a synopsis of our major positions, discussed in greater detail in the individual chapters.

Commodities (Chapter 2)

World price supports for primary-product exports constitute the keystone of NIEO. It is the proposition most discussed in the literature and most negotiated at international conferences, such as UNCTAD, and in the North-South dialogues.

The "catch" here, as we have already explained, is that the rich (in both poor and rich countries) are the producers of the primary products but the poor spend a higher proportion of their incomes on the consumption of those products than do the rich. Therefore, higher prices for primary products would be a burden to the poor everywhere, and the rich would benefit. The gainers would also include the multinational corporations.

Two other points are pertinent.

First, the proposition that the terms of trade move against LDCs has not been substantiated. All studies that have "demonstrated" the proposition have been based on selective perception, including the selection of years when primary-product prices were declining and not considering years in which the prices were rising; the selection of products whose prices have fallen because of technological obsolescence and excluding those whose prices were rising; or the selection of some countries and not others. When all countries, all products, and all years are analyzed, no long-term pattern, either of increase or decrease, is discernible.

Second, economic development historically occurs in an environment of improved technology, decreased prices, and increased exports. At the same time, a truly developing country diversifies away from primary products and into manufacturing. NIEO is part of a contrary environment, in which LDC governments seek protected markets, higher prices, and decreased exports and pay little attention to experimentation and technology.

Trade Reform and the Generalized System of Preferences (Chapter 3)

The Generalized System of Preferences (GSP) requires MDCs to admit the products of LDCs either duty free or at preferential rates, but LDCs do not accord the same privileges to MDCs. LDCs are presumed to need such preferences in order to compete against the more efficient producers in the MDCs; and for the same reason, they should not grant reciprocal preferences to the MDC producers.

The "catch" is that if LDCs expand their exports, they must also expand their imports. Only in countries that give foreign aid or invest abroad can exports exceed imports. In other countries, any increases in exports must be equaled by increases in imports. If they are not, these countries would simply accumulate foreign exchange (which does them no good if not spent).

If LDCs increase their exports through GSP, what will they do with the foreign exchange? If they continue to keep their own duties high, then the rich people who own the export potential will probably spend the new foreign exchange on luxury imports for their own consumption, or else on machinery so that they can manufacture the goods that are not imported because of high duties. If the latter, then they will produce manufactured goods to sell to their fellow citizens at high, protected prices. Having excluded the poor from buying manufactured goods abroad at lower prices, they would force them to buy at higher prices from the producers (the rich). In this way, income is once more transferred from poor to rich.

The GSP has now been in effect for at least half a decade, and we are able to measure some of its results. We find the greatest benefit to the poor has occurred in ten countries whose governments have *not* behaved in the manner described in the preceding paragraph. Known as newly industrializing countries (NICs), this group accomplished two goals simultaneously: (1) They increased their own access to MDC markets, and (2) by reducing their own protection, they developed efficient home industries, which could sell to their nationals at prices lower than those of exporters from MDCs. The NICs' success disproves the allegation that to survive, LDC manufacturers require heavy protection against "efficient" MDC producers. Furthermore, the percentage of absolute poor (those on the edge of starvation) in these ten NICs is far lower than in the much larger group of LDCs that insist on high protection for their own manufacturers.

In summary, the LDCs that have been most successful in both per capita economic growth and reduction of poverty have been those that relied on GSP only in part, but went on to negotiate their way into the markets of MDCs.

We favor GSP. The encouragement that it gives to labor-intensive exports of LDCs is likely to help both employment and wages. GSP as a means of promoting exports is perhaps the next best thing to LDC bargaining in the international market, through an international agency such as the General Agreement on Tariffs and Trade (GATT).

But we do not deem it wise for LDCs to give up the "best thing" (free trade) in favor of the "next best" (preferential trade). It also does not appear realistic to extend the commodity coverage of GSP, for MDC governments are not likely to agree. Rather, we propose two steps: first, that LDCs increase the acceptability of their exports abroad through bargaining within the GATT, and second, that NICs and MDCs jointly extend GSP to the least developed countries (LDLDCs). Thus the cycle would be repeated.

Multinational Corporations (Chapter 4)

The NIEO proposes an international code of conduct to regulate the practices of multinational corporations (MNCs), which are depicted as powerful world groups that are able to manipulate LDC policies in their favor.

The "catch" is that virtually all the unsavory tactics of MNCs are also practiced by large companies of national origin. We see the campaign against MNCs as an inadvertent alliance between the most reactionary elements in the LDCs—people who would muzzle MNCs so that they themselves can assume the monopoly—and liberals concerned that no one should have too much power. Unfortunately, the liberals have neglected the powerful locals. If domestic companies produce less efficiently than MNCs, then controls on MNCs may well lead to higher prices for manufactured goods, which would further burden the LDC poor.

We believe in equality before the law. We do not mean the law that equally forbids rich and poor to sleep under bridges; we do mean the law that controls the conduct of large companies, domestic and foreign. Unconscionable practices should be outlawed. We favor a code of business behavior, not a code that is applicable to some companies and exempts others.

Chapter 4 analyzes sixteen charges frequently made against MNCs. When these charges are taken one by one, it appears that MNCs are far less formidable than is their reputation in the aggregate. Virtually all their unsavory practices are already either controlled by LDC governments or lie within their potential control. In countries where the governments have not exercised control, it is because they do not want to. NIEO does not propose international control but an international code, to be enforced at the pleasure of local governments. To us, this would be the fox tending the chicken coop.

Some of the charges against MNCs cannot be substantiated. Contrary to much popular belief, they pay higher wages on an average and provide more comfortable working conditions than do domestic companies. In some cases, their behavior is a normal response to policies (many of them inefficient) set by the host government.

The gains that have already been made by many LDC governments also belie the pervasive power of the MNCs. LDC governments have nationalized virtually all petroleum companies and most other mineral producers; they have taxed away most of the earnings of many MNCs; and they have successfully controlled prices, employment and wage practices, lending practices, and currency exchanges.

We question the proposition that technology should be transferred more freely from MDCs to LDCs. MDC technology has been, in general, designed for large-scale, capital-intensive enterprises, and most of it would not be appropriate in LDCs. Inappropriate technological choices must then be validated by policy controls favoring the owners of enterprises. Since these controls invariably increase prices, they are disadvantageous to the poor. We also question whether ready technology transfer from MDCs would not discourage the development of research in LDCs.

International Monetary Reform (Chapter 5)

The NIEO proposes that LDCs should have greater influence over the international monetary system (IMS). This system, which evolved through international agreements such as those made at Bretton Woods (1944) and Jamaica (1976), determines the rules for international currencies and how the international money supply shall be augmented.

The "catch" is inflation. In any monetary system (national or international), new money must be created as output rises. If the world money supply increases in the same proportion as world output, then (other things being equal) there will be no inflation. This happy state of affairs would require that new money be created in a neutral way so as not to upset the existing money distribution. Inflation occurs when some groups, with easier access to credit than others, cause new money to be created to their special advantage. This situation has occurred in MDCs and LDCs—it also occurred during the time of the Roman Empire, during the reign of Henry VIII in England, and at many other times in history.

International money consists of certain key currencies—such as the dollar and the pound—plus gold, plus the new SDRs issued by the IMF. The NIEO proposes that SDRs should be issued preferentially to poor countries. In this way, the monetary system would become a legitimate instrument for transferring resources from one group to another. But for centuries, the monetary system has been used illegitimately for such transfers—and they have inevitably led to inflation. We fear that legitimizing them would be to legitimize worldwide inflation, however laudatory the objective of transferring wealth from rich to poor. And even that laudatory objective probably would not be realized, for the new SDRs would not be doled out to the poor at all. They would go to rich people in poor countries.

Special issues of SDRs to LDC governments are a means of foreign aid. The LDC governments would be given the right to buy whatever resources they chose in MDCs, but if they chose to use the SDRs to buy luxury consumption goods for their rich, then nothing would be added to world production. The new money would become directly inflationary, raising prices paid by poor people everywhere. This is one more way in which wealth can be transferred from the poor to the rich. There should be assurances against this unhappy outcome before new governments are admitted to the rule-making process, but everything we have seen in the NIEO literature leads us to believe that LDC governments would have no intention of making such assurances. It seems to us that other means of foreign aid have a greater probability of directly helping the poor.

Debt (Chapter 6)

Over the past decade, the debts of LDC governments and LDC private institutions mounted enormously. Much of the increase was due to the high price of oil, but a large part of it was caused by corruption and mismanagement of government resources. NIEO proposes, as a way to transfer resources from rich to poor, that this debt should be renegotiated, rescheduled, or canceled at least in part. Some MDC governments have already canceled small portions of the debt due them.

There are two "catches" here. The first is that one has to be relatively rich to borrow in the first place; poor people can't borrow. Thus, debt cancellation is mostly a form of aid to the rich. The second "catch" is that the principal beneficiaries would be banks in New York, California, and Europe. These banks may have overextended themselves in lending to LDCs, and if the bank loans were canceled, presumably the lending banks' governments would provide compensation. That would make the banks happy, just as the Chrysler Corporation's creditors were happy when the U.S. government guaranteed that company's indebtedness.

We are also uncomfortable about legitimizing debt cancellation as a regular feature of an international order. Credit is the lifeblood of the world economy. If periodic cancellations are envisaged, capital will not flow freely except with government guarantees. Besides being inflationary, such guarantees would imply a business-government relationship that might be stronger than would be desirable.

Finally, the debts incurred by third world countries are still manageable in that the countries can utilize their exports to service those debts. Severe debt problems, such as in Turkey and Peru, have been caused by financial mismanagement, and particular aspects of mismanagement can be identified and cured if governments are willing. Perhaps their willingness to do so would be encouraged if they were not bailed out periodically by international action.

Oil, Debt, Trade, and Growth (Chapter 7)

The increases in petroleum prices since 1973 have been widely touted as meaning a massive transfer of wealth from rich to poor, but they have meant nothing of the sort. The primary beneficiaries have been those who were already rich by any standard, and the world's poor have suffered far more than the world's rich. The price of oil has gone up for everyone, but most of the world's poor are consumers or potential consumers of oil; only a very few are producers. The increased cost of petrochemical fertilizers has thus worked great hardship on small-scale farmers in the third world.

Of course, rich customers in MDCs also pay more for oil, but by and large, the money has come back to their countries. With their newfound riches, oil producers have tended to buy more from the rich countries (because they have more interesting goods to offer); the producers have invested primarily in those same countries (because they offer better investment opportunities); and what the producers have left over, they have deposited in banks and government securities in the industrialized countries (because their money is safer there). Thus, although rich and poor have both paid more to the Organization of Petroleum Exporting Countries (OPEC), those countries have spent, invested, and deposited funds primarily in rich countries. Therefore, the net flow of wealth has been from poor countries, via OPEC, to rich ones.

Other Provisions (Chapter 8)

Food Production. We strongly agree that there should be "concrete measures to increase food production and storage facilities in developing countries." We also would support an international food reserve (curiously omitted from the NIEO plan) to prevent starvation during famine periods.

However, governments in most LDCs have long discriminated against agriculture, and they have systematically neglected the poorer, small-scale farmers. It does not seem right that governments that have refused to promote small-scale agriculture should somehow expect an international order to rescue them—especially when elsewhere in the document, those governments strongly assert their desire for independence.

Foreign Aid. The NIEO asks that MDCs increase financial aid to LDCs. But foreign aid always comes conditionally and will never be proffered in significant quantities in ways that may damage the interests of MDCs. Aid may help poor farmers—and that is all to the good—for they do not threaten the efficient agricultural enterprises of the MDCs. But little aid has been given, or is likely to be given, for manufacturing in LDCs. If the peoples of the LDCs wish to decrease their dependence on decisions made abroad, they need to reduce their dependence on foreign aid.

Foreign Investment. While proposing an international code of conduct to govern the behavior of multinational corporations, NIEO also seeks increased foreign investment. Apparently, the authors of the plan desire greater loans from international institutions such as the World Bank as well as increased control over the proceeds.

We question the realism of this proposal. Any funds received from the World Bank will have the careful scrutiny of the U.S. Congress—those who would change that part of the old order might just as well try to shift the orbit of the moon. If LDCs wish to free themselves of foreign controls over investment, they should obtain their capital at market terms instead of through preferential channels, which are always laden with conditions.

LDCs' Share in Industrial Production. The share of LDCs in world manufacturing exports, long stagnant or declining, has taken a remarkable upturn during the seventies and early eighties, and a further increase is to be encouraged. However, we believe that success lies squarely within the power of LDC governments and manufacturers and that it depends, not on an international order, but on quality exports capable of competing in price. We have already suggested (in conjunction with GSP) that those people who believe that LDC producers are unable to find their way into the international market have unrealistically disparaged the capabilities of those producers.

The Internal Gap (Chaper 9)

While proposing reforms of international institutions, LDC governments have neglected reforms at home. With only a few exceptions, LDC governments promote modern industry and modern agriculture at the expense of traditional occupations and rural people. The LDC governments concentrate infrastructure and education in urban, modern areas, so they become more accessible to the rich than to the poor; they allow low interest rates and preferential access to credit, policies that favor the rich; they overvalue exchange rates, thus helping industries in the modern sector at the expense of traditional employment; they favor modern industries with heavy tariff protection, which increases prices paid by the poor; they subsidize modern industries and give them tax breaks, which encourages capital-intensive investment; they protect urban labor unions, increasing the wages of a select few workers and thus causing unemployment for the many people who do not belong to the union; and they fail to collect taxes efficiently, so that burdens fall disproportionately on the consuming poor.

Although we do not believe that the planners of the NIEO so intended, we think NIEO has turned out to be a smokescreen that draws attention away from the need for internal reforms. Furthermore, all the international privileges demanded by NIEO (higher prices for commodity exports, debt cancellation, and greater foreign aid and investment) would favor the modern sector disproportionately and make the poor worse off.

We conclude that the road to equitable economic growth lies in improved scientific and managerial capabilities, productivity, and trade, especially among the poorest people in the LDCs. Those people who believe that this road is closed, or even severely encumbered, have not examined all opportunities, have interpreted them with too much pessimism, or have unfairly underestimated the potential of the poor. By contrast, NIEO is an illusory set of vaguely expressed concepts that, if implemented, would most likely retard economic growth and redistribute resources from poor to rich. Institutional change, which is needed more seriously within LDCs than internationally, will come about only through bargaining, by the poor, from positions of strength.

Bibliography

Brandt Commission. *North-South Program for Survival*. Cambridge, Mass.: MIT Press, 1980.

United Nations Conference on Trade and Development (UNCTAD 1). *Proceedings*, vol. 1, *Final Act and Report*. E/CONF. 46/141. Geneva, 1964.

2
Commodities

When the delegates assembled at the first Conference on International Economic Cooperation at Paris in December 1975, the mood was one of guarded conflict. The North—represented by the United States, Japan, the European Economic Community (EEC), and five other MDCs— looked on the conference as a way of negotiating a better deal on oil prices. They hoped to split the South into NOPECs (non-oil-exporting LDCs) and OPEC and to draw the NOPECs to their side. After all, NOPECs had suffered more from the increased price of oil than had the countries of the North. The NOPECs, on the other hand, believed their political advantage lay in a continued alliance with OPEC. Not only did they feel greater cultural affinity in such an alliance, but they admired OPEC for achieving what they had long tried to do: force the North to pay higher prices for their primary-product exports.

The North-South dialogues have proceeded in a desultory fashion for over half a decade. Along with NIEO, these dialogues have been the subject of numerous books. Bulletins from the United Nations and writings of religious organizations in Europe and North America favor the South on grounds of morality and equity. Many writers blame the North for the delays in the reform, and some say that once it became clear that the dialogues would have little effect on the price of oil, the North lost interest.

Those writers look on NIEO as an inevitable extension of the historical sequence of political independence and greater strength for the third world, but we view it as a reversal of the historical trend. The history of the past three centuries is one of increased productive efficiency and a more rational deployment of resources, so as to reduce costs and pass benefits on to consumers—and in the process, to liberalize trade and improve the distribution of income. Benefits have increased for rich and poor alike. NIEO, on the other hand, represents a philosophy of cartelization and restriction of output with greater governmental controls.

This divergence in philosophy is the key to our disagreement with

NIEO advocates. It therefore deserves detailed examination in connection with specific points. Let us begin with NIEO proposals to support the prices of primary-product exports.

Indexing Prices:
Primary Products to Manufactured Goods

At the Paris meeting in 1975, the South was united in favoring a plan to tie the prices of primary-product exports to those of industrial goods. Primary products are products of the soil before processing. They can be agricultural or mineral. They constitute the principal exports of third world countries. For many years, economists and diplomats from those countries have complained that the prices of their primary exports persistently and secularly tend to decline in relation to the prices of their industrial imports. As a result, as time goes on, they believe that a given quantity of imports costs more and more in terms of exports. In a 1976 article, President Nyerere of Tanzania complained that "in 1965 I could buy a tractor by selling 15.25 tons of sisal. The price of the same model in 1972 needed 42 tons of sisal." (p. 4)

To prevent this decline from continuing in the future, the South has proposed that there be an international agreement to increase the price of a primary product when its price does not rise in the same proportion as the average price for internationally traded industrial goods. For example, if industrial prices rise by 10 percent, but the price of copper increases by only 4 percent, then an international arrangement should assure that copper would rise by 6 percent more. The process is known as indexing the price of copper to the prices of industrial goods.

Exactly how indexing would be achieved is not yet clear, but there are several possibilities. Governments of industrial countries might add the extra 6 percent as a subsidy, or all governments might agree to price control. It would be illegal to sell copper anywhere in the world except at the full 10 percent increase. Alternatively, copper companies might agree to limit output, so that the price would rise of its own accord. In the latter case, governments of consuming countries would have to limit imports; otherwise illicit sellers might undercut the agreements.

Of course, governments will not agree on the mechanisms if they disagree on the concept, and therein lies the rub. First, there is no agreement that the original premise is true. Many people believe that the prices of primary products do not decline, over time, in relation to those of industrial goods. Second, indexing the prices of some goods in terms of the prices of other goods creates so many inefficiencies that the process won't work. Let us consider relative prices first; we will return to the second point later in this chapter.

The Terms of Trade

The relationship between the prices of what one buys and what one sells is known, technically, as the "terms of trade." For example, Tanzania sells sisal and buys U.S. tractors. Suppose that in a given year (call it the base year), sisal sells for $160 per ton and a given model of tractor sells for $10,000. Suppose that in a subsequent year (call it the given year), the price of sisal falls to $120 per ton and the price of the tractor rises to $11,000. The terms of trade become 75/110. The price of sisal is in the numerator, which shows the price to be 75 percent of what it was in the base year. The price of tractors is in the denominator, where it registers 110 percent. The fraction, 75/110, equals .68, so the terms of trade for Tanzanian sisal versus U.S. tractors have fallen from 1.0 to .68. Since it is more convenient not to worry about decimals, we will say they have fallen from 100 to 68. Since Nyerere complained that he had to pay 2.75 as much sisal for the same tractor, he was saying that the terms of trade had deteriorated for Tanzania to 36 (since 1/ 2.75 = .36). The terms of trade are always 100 in the base year, to which the given year is compared.

Now, the proposition that primary-export prices should be indexed to those of industrial exports must be predicated on the earlier thesis that over time, the terms of trade deteriorate for primary producers. If that thesis were not true—for example, if the two sets of prices varied randomly with respect to each other—then pegging would cause the South to lose half the time and gain the other half. All the costly procedures for setting international prices would be for naught, for everything would balance out in the end. Therefore, we must conclude that the South believes in the deterioration thesis, and the fact that they do is evident from the many times the thesis has been voiced at international conferences and in proposals for a NIEO.

But, actually, there is no empirical basis for the deterioration thesis. If the prices of all primary products and all industrial goods are examined over a long period of time, they will be seen to vary widely with respect to each other, but no persistent trend is discernible, one way or the other. For simplicity, we will hereafter refer to the deterioration thesis as "the belief" and we begin by asking, How did "the belief" become so widespread?

The fact is that we do not accept "the belief." We think, rather, that it is one of those propositions that is almost universally believed and that turns out to be false. Among such propositions are the intellectual superiority of some race, magical explanations of physical phenomena, and the Ptolemaic theory of the universe. In all such cases, two factors were present. First, the explanation made apparent sense. Second, large numbers of people wanted to believe it.

We believe these conditions are also present for the terms-of-trade depreciation theory. Superficially, "the belief" makes sense. As the world industrializes, manufacturing makes up a greater percentage of the world output, and primary products make up a smaller percentage. As a consequence, the prices of primary products must fall. (But if this theory were true, the prices of gold and silver should long since have reached close to zero.) But in addition to its apparent sense, politicians and economists from the third world and their supporters in industrialized countries want very much to believe the deterioration thesis.

How "the Belief" Came About

Before 1948, no one to our knowledge had made any serious suggestion that the terms of trade tend to deteriorate persistently for primary products. In 1945, with no thought for the terms of trade, the League of Nations had done a study on the role of industrialization in foreign trade. As a step in calculating the relative values of manufactures and primary products, the League of Nations had estimated price series for British imports and exports from 1876 to 1938. Argentine economist Raul Prebisch, the first executive director of the UN Economic Commission for Latin America, incorporated these series in his landmark paper, *The Economic Development of Latin America and Its Principal Problems* (UN, ECLA 1950, republished as Prebisch 1962). This paper proclaimed that the terms of trade for primary products had deteriorated to 64.1 in 1936–1938, compared to the base period 1876–1880. So as not to end with a depression year, Prebisch added his own calculation of 68.7 for 1946–1947. He believed there had been an almost persistent deterioration for well over half a century.

Within a few years, other economists found errors in Prebisch's methods. First, he had used only British data, and the British had included transportation costs in the prices of their imports but not in those of their exports. Ellsworth (1956) noted that from 1886 to 1905, a technological revolution in shipping had lowered transport costs significantly, and thus, the decreased prices the British were paying for imports were really decreases in transport rates. When adjustment was made for this fact, Ellsworth calculated that the terms of trade were actually deteriorating for Britain and improving for its trading partners in the third world. From 1913 on, Ellsworth admitted that the terms of trade might be deteriorating for Britain's trading partners, but he found the declines to be associated with specific, passing events, such as wartime controls and depression, rather than with any persistent tendency.

Second, in looking only at British prices, Prebisch had not considered the prices of other industrial exporters. A French economist, Bairoch (1975), estimated that had Prebisch studied data for U.S. exports, the terms of trade would have deteriorated much less for the third world, and had he used data for continental Europe, they would have improved. If third world countries had bought their manufactured goods from countries whose prices were the cheapest, they would have been switching from Britain to other areas, and their terms of trade would have improved.

Two other studies of similar magnitude were made at approximately the same time. One, by Lewis (1952), analyzed the composition of world production and, incidentally, produced an index of terms of trade for primary products versus manufactures. The Lewis data showed many ups and downs but no significant overall trend. In 1950, the terms of trade were just about where they had been in 1871. The other study, by Kindleberger (1956), focused on continental European prices vis-à-vis the less developed world. Kindleberger concluded that "there is no long-run tendency for the terms of trade to move against primary products in favor of manufactures" (p. 236).

John Spraos (1980) has surveyed competing arguments in light of data generated through the 1970s. He shows that Prebisch's calculations greatly exaggerated the deterioration in terms of trade that he found. Furthermore, compared to price trends before World War II, more recent primary-product prices have "done quite well."

Therefore, for studies of the prewar period, the score stands as follows: three (by Lewis and Kindleberger and Spraos) show no long-run change in the terms of trade between primary products and manufactures, and one (by Prebisch) shows deterioration for primary products. When other economists have corrected errors discovered in the original Prebisch work, that deterioration vanishes.

Any study of the terms of trade before World War II requires special research, since third world countries did not gather many statistics until later. Since 1950, however, most governments have collected information on the prices of their imports and exports, commodity by commodity. Because the original Prebisch study was published in 1950, it could not take this information into account and had to contend with the statistical situation of its day.

Now that more statistics are available, what does more than thirty years of postwar experience tell us? It tells us unequivocally that the terms of trade are not observed to deteriorate for primary products in the long run. This conclusion is substantiated by a number of agencies, as follows.

1. In the early postwar years, the United Nations began preparing terms-of-trade indexes for less developed countries, and the UN Economic Commission for Latin America (ECLA) did so for Latin American countries until 1973. We have spliced the indexes together, and the results are shown in Figure 2.1. Although based on price data originally prepared by the very governments whose diplomats pronounce "the belief," the figure shows no evidence of any trend, one way or another.

2. In 1974, the secretary general of the United Nations Conference on Trade and Development (Gamani Corea of Sri Lanka) invited experts from both MDCs and LDCs to prepare a report on the feasibility of indexing primary-product prices to those of manufactured goods (Dale 1975). That report stated, "There was general agreement that the statistics presented to the group did not provide any clear evidence of a long-term deterioration in the terms of trade of developing countries, although they did suggest that these terms of trade were subject to substantial short-term fluctuations."

3. The International Monetary Fund, which continued the terms-of-trade reporting during the seventies, found no persistent trend from 1962 to 1979. According to the IMF *Annual Report* (1980, p. 17), prices of manufactured goods in world trade rose by 210 percent during that period, and those of non-oil primary products rose by 216 percent (the difference is probably insignificant, statistically). Since the price of oil rose by 1,187 percent during the same period, the terms of trade of both MDCs and NOPECs fell, to 89 for the former and 83 for the latter (1962 = 100); for OPEC, they improved to 245. Since NOPECs' terms of trade with the industrial countries were about the same in 1979 as in 1962, their terms of trade must have deteriorated in relation to those of OPEC more than those of the industrial countries did.

Selective Perception

How, then, is "the belief" supported? What data do the diplomats cite in the North-South dialogues? The examples are all selectively perceived. Commodities whose prices have deteriorated because of special circumstances may be chosen and others whose prices have risen may be neglected. Or, time periods of falling prices may be chosen and not those in which prices were rising.

Selective Perception by Commodity. President Nyerere's statement on sisal was selective perception by commodity. Sisal had been threatened by nylon and other synthetic materials in the manufacture of cord and thread, so it is not surprising that its price was going down. Had Nyerere chosen a different export of his country, tea, he might have shown that the terms of trade had appreciated for Tanzanian tea versus U.S.

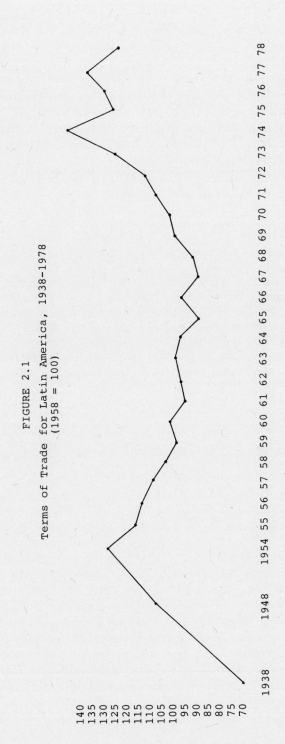

FIGURE 2.1

Terms of Trade for Latin America, 1938-1978
(1958 = 100)

The only official terms-of-trade series we could find for LDCs, covering a forty-year period, was published for Latin America by the United Nations. We had to splice three indices together from UN Statistical Yearbook, 1964, p. 485; UN Statistical Bulletin for Latin America, Vol. VIII, No. 2, 1971, p. 93, and UN Statistical Yearbook for Latin America, 1978, pp. 342-343. For the years for which data were published for all less developed countries, or for primary-product exports, the movements were roughly parallel; hence this series is probably representative. Nevertheless, all indices of this nature are averages and should be interpreted with caution.

manufactured goods to 975 in 1977, compared to base year 1969 (IMF 1979).

Selective Perception by Years. The second kind of selective perception is by time period (see Figure 2.2). To take the example of Tanzanian sisal again, in a remarkable recovery, its price sextupled from 1970 to 1976, so President Nyerere's comment might have been quite different if he had used a later date. One can make almost any case one wishes, if only one chooses the years properly!

As early as 1967, Bauer pointed out the selective perception by the United Nations.

> The easiest way to arrange statistics to show a long-term or systematic deterioration of the terms of trade is simply to omit the years over which they have improved, a device frequently employed in UN-UNCTAD discussions. The alleged secular decline in the terms of trade of under-developed countries was first widely publicised in UN literature on the basis of a series beginning with the 1870s and ending in 1938; in the Prebisch Report and the UNCTAD literature it is derived from a series beginning in 1950 and terminating with 1961. Between 1938 and 1950 the commodity terms of trade of primary producers improved by almost two-fifths, even without any correction for the improvement in the quality of manufactures. It is easy to assert that the terms of trade of primary producers always decline if the years when they have risen are omitted. [Bauer 1971, pp. 253–54]

In Figure 2.1, we see the terms of trade for Latin America rising strongly from 1938 to 1954, then falling until about 1965, then rising again. Many speeches in the United Nations have pointed out the significant declines in the terms of trade from approximately 1950–1954 to approximately 1965. From 1950 to 1954, raw materials prices were at an all-time high, first because of the Korean War and then because of a series of frosts in coffee areas. But if a different period were selected, say 1940–1955, or 1963–1973, the data would show the terms of trade improving for primary producers. Selective perception by commodity and by years may, of course, be combined.

The Theory Behind "the Belief"

To be credible among social scientists, every empirical event must have a theoretical explanation. When Prebisch presented his study on the terms of trade, he was aware that his results contradicted classical economic theory. Therefore, he had to tell why he felt classical theory was wrong, and he had to substitute his own theory. Let us now review the classical theory and Prebisch's revisions.

Classical Theory of the Terms of Trade. Economists have long believed

FIGURE 2.2

Selective Perception by the United Nations:
Indices of Prices of Industrial Production and Primary Producing Countries, 1950-1959

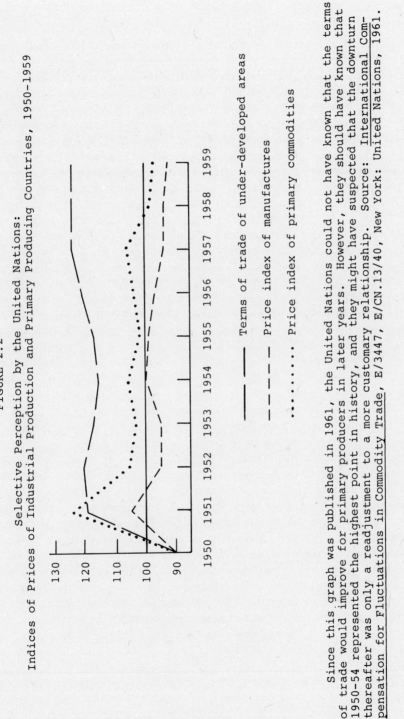

——————— Terms of trade of under-developed areas

— — — — Price index of manufactures

· · · · · · · · Price index of primary commodities

Since this graph was published in 1961, the United Nations could not have known that the terms of trade would improve for primary producers in later years. However, they should have known that 1950-54 represented the highest point in history, and they might have suspected that the downturn thereafter was only a readjustment to a more customary relationship. Source: International Compensation for Fluctuations in Commodity Trade, E/3447, E/CN.13/40, New York: United Nations, 1961.

that the terms of trade would worsen for countries that increase their productivity in relation to other countries. As Europe and North America developed during the nineteenth and twentieth centuries, they could export their products more and more cheaply relative to the prices they paid for imports.

One reason, of course, was that they could produce more cheaply and competition drove their prices down. But a fall in prices need not depend on competition. Suppose the United States produces automobiles, Egypt produces cotton, and there is a certain exchange rate (so much cotton for an automobile). Suppose the United States increases its productivity so that the same amount of capital and labor can now produce more automobiles than before, and productivity remains un-changed in Egypt. In real terms, the Americans' income has risen. If the Americans decide to spend the entire income increment on auto-mobiles, then there will be no change in the terms of trade with Egypt. (The Egyptians won't even know what happened.) But if the Americans decide that with higher incomes, they want to buy more cotton as well, then they must lower the price of automobiles (in terms of cotton) to persuade the Egyptians to sell more cotton in exchange. The Americans will be better off because of their income increase, but the Egyptians will be better off too because the price of automobiles has declined. By wanting more cotton, the Americans are required to share some of their productivity increase with the Egyptians. It does not matter whether either or both of them operate in competition or in monopoly.

Prebisch's Theory of the Terms of Trade. However, Prebisch believed that the classical theory depended only on competition. Only when there is competition, he said, will decreased costs be passed on to the consumer in the form of lower prices because monopolies will not allow prices to go down just because productivity has increased. Instead, they will increase wages and profits. Powerful labor unions contribute to this decision. Because the industrialized world is becoming more and more monopolized, Prebisch reasoned that less and less does it share its productivity gains with the third world.

There are, in fact, two errors in Prebisch's theory. The first is that even if his basic reasoning were correct, he has not explained why the terms of trade have *deteriorated* for the third world; he has only explained why they did not improve as classical theory said they should. Second, he has ignored the point that classical theory already takes account of monopoly, showing that productivity gains will be shared under either condition.

How would this sharing occur? Suppose U.S. automobile producers did decide not to lower their prices in the face of productivity increases, but instead decided to pay the entire increment to their workers and their stockholders. In that case, they would not sell more cars to the Egyptians unless cars became cheaper for Egyptians in some other way. That other way would be via the exchange rate. If Americans, with their higher incomes, decided they wanted to buy more cotton, they would bid up the price of the Egyptian pound. The ensuing depreciation of the dollar would give the Egyptians the advantage that classical theory assigns them. (The Prebisch argument does not include consideration of the exchange rate.)

For people who might be confused by seeing the price of automobiles perpetually rising (like everything else), we explain that we are theorizing in terms of *real* prices, which are relative to the inflation rate. The real price of some good rises only if the money price increases by more than the general price index. Conversely, a real price declines when the money price rises by less than the general price index.

How can the classical theory be checked against empirical evidence? Unfortunately, it cannot. So many other factors, such as different rates of inflation in different countries, affect prices and exchange rates that one cannot prove, directly, that the classical theory is correct or incorrect. All we can do is point out that there is no logical error in it, whereas there is a logical error in Prebisch's theory, and we have already presented what we believe is convincing empirical evidence that the terms of trade do not in fact deteriorate persistently and secularly for producers of primary products.

Furthermore, neither Prebisch nor anyone else (to our knowledge) has ever refuted the professional objections to either his empirical study or his theory.[1] In most economics disputes, there will be point and counterpoint, and the *American Economic Review* will publish both sides of a debate that may continue for several issues. In the case of the terms of trade, however, the argument just died. Perhaps—like the Ptolemaic theory of the universe—there was no need to answer objections. "The belief" was already widely and tenaciously held!

Why Not Raise Prices Anyway?

Even if the terms of trade have not been moving, secularly, against primary producers, why shouldn't those producers raise their prices anyway? Don't the poor countries need assistance? Some say they have been wronged in the past, and increased prices would be a means of redress.

The answer is, first, that higher prices of primary products would not transfer income from the rich to the poor, most likely the transfer would be the other way around. Second, if transfer to the poor is what is wanted, there are more efficient ways of doing it. And finally, we suggest that cartelization and monopoly—which commodity price agreements would require—are not the most effective ways of economic development.

Income Transfers: Poor to Rich

Accompanying "the belief" has been the idea that the poor are the producers of primary products that they sell to the rich who pay for them with manufactured goods. But this simple proposition is far from the truth. Many rich countries also produce primary products. The United States produces 75 percent of the copper it consumes, for example, so if the price of copper were increased in the world market, a few U.S. MNCs would be principal gainers. In fact, more than half the world's exports of primary products comes from rich countries, not poor ones.

Furthermore, increases in primary-product prices inevitably cause increases in the prices of manufactured goods, which the poor consume. A higher price for copper will cause the price of copper wiring and pipes to go up, making decent housing more costly for the poor.

Increasing the prices of primary products is like putting a tax on them and paying the proceeds to the producers. It has long been known that taxes on commodities (like sales and excise taxes) are regressive in that they burden the poor more, relatively, than they do the rich, because the poor must spend a greater percentage of their income on goods. In general, the producers of primary products in the third world are not the poorest people in a country. They are likely to be wealthy plantation owners, private companies owned by rich people, or government companies that pay excessive salaries to their officials and are not known for distributing their profits to the poor. The beneficiaries are even likely to be MNCs owned by stockholders in the first world.

Nor are the countries that export primary products generally among the poorest countries (even apart from those in OPEC). Brazil with its coffee, Chile with its copper, and Argentina with its cattle are among the richest in the third world. There are—we must say in counterargument—some poor countries among the primary producers: Botswana, Bolivia, and Zambia, for example. But in each of those latter cases (which must be examined separately), the poverty is explainable more by internal inefficiencies than by low prices. The real losers from NIEO could be the poor countries without heavy primary exports—like Mali, Chad, Papua New Guinea, and Haiti. Those are the forgotten countries.

There is another reason why the poor would suffer. Artificially increased prices imply restrictions in production, and although, for the most part, the poor are not the owners of assets in primary production, in a few cases they are. In coffee-producing countries, for example, there are both large plantations (owned by the wealthy) and small farms (sometimes owned by the poor). When the government of a coffee-producing country must decide whose production will be restricted, can we presume that they will constrain the rich before they do the poor, or even restrict each in equal proportion?

Efficient Versus Inefficient Transfers

We join the advocates of NIEO in supporting transfers of resources from the rich to the poor. But there are efficient and inefficient ways to do so. The case of pocket calculators shows why indexing is an inefficient way.

Over the last ten years, the terms of trade for pocket calculators have deteriorated from 100 to about 2. A calculator costing $200 ten years ago would sell for about $10 now, even though the prices of its inputs may have more than doubled. Why are calculators cheaper? Because some of the costs have gone down while the market has expanded. Suppose, however, that the price of calculators had been indexed to the consumer price index. In that case, the producers of the $200 calculator in 1970 would have been required by law to sell the same calculator for $433.19 in October 1980—presumably to protect the producer from the ill effects of falling prices. One can imagine the result: The producer might go bankrupt because fewer people would be able to afford to buy pocket calculators!

But, our critics might say, primary products are different from pocket calculators. One cannot increase the productivity (output per dollar of cost) of primary products the way one can of manufactured goods. However, improvements in agricultural productivity in the United States since the 1930s have been enormous, and the output of some crops has increased by more than five times per unit of land and labor. The green revolution has provided similar results in the third world. (In several countries, the benefits of the green revolution have been enjoyed more by the rich than by the poor, but this is the result of internal policies, not of international pricing.) The past half century has also seen cost-reducing innovations in the production of most minerals.

In summary, prices of different goods should change according to changes in technology, the skill of the producers, capital investment, consumer demand, and the like. If any one good is indexed to the price of another, the producer of the indexed good may be required to offer his product at prices that are either too high to allow his full output to be sold or too low to cover his costs.

The indexing of primary-product prices to manufactured goods is therefore an inefficient, and likely unsuccessful, way to transfer income from rich to poor. What way would be more efficient? The answer is simple: taxing the income and wealth of the rich, in both MDCs and LDCs, and disbursing the revenue for the betterment of the poor or else paying it to them outright. The taxation would not be regressive (as increased commodity prices would be), and the benefits would not go to the rich (as increased commodity prices probably would).

Why do third world diplomats not ask for this solution, instead of commodity price indexing? They do ask for increased foreign aid, but they do not propose (in NIEO) that that aid go primarily to their countries' poor. But we also suspect that the diplomats, who are usually among the rich in their own countries, are looking for transfers that they themselves can control and benefit from. For the most part, the rich own or control the productive facilities of the primary goods.

Possibly critics will tell us that direct transfers from the rich (anywhere in the world) to the poor (anywhere in the world) are less likely, politically, than commodity indexing. We see no sign that this probability is so. Indeed, if we must choose between two objectives that are equally infeasible politically, we prefer to struggle for the better one, for it will have a greater chance of being ultimately accepted when the climate of opinion changes.

The General Philosophy: Centralization vs. Dispersion of Power

Advocates of NIEO generally condemn cartelization and monopoly when they occur in industrialized countries or through MNCs. They also oppose government-business combinations (some of which are derogatorily called part of the "military-industrial complex"). Yet these same advocates would propose that cartels, monopolies, price increases, and restrictions in production should be built into the international order.

Perhaps these advocates might observe that, historically, the underdog of one era has become the superlord of another. Should they not be concerned about dispersal, rather than concentration, of power, no matter who holds it?

Historically, the key to overcoming poverty has lain in increased rather than in decreased production, the overcoming of monopolies rather than creating more, and the reduction of costs and prices. When a country is successful in all of these endeavors, the terms of trade move *against* it, not in its favor.

Fluctuations in Prices: A Different Problem

The wording of the Declaration of the NIEO obscures the presence of two debates on the prices of primary products. One concerns the alleged deterioration in the terms of trade. The other concerns the wide fluctuations in prices of primary products over the business cycle. The confusion of these distinct questions has considerably muddied the NIEO waters.

The prices of primary products regularly fluctuate more, over the business cycle, than do those of manufactured goods. As manufacturing prices rise, primary prices rise more; as the former fall, the latter fall further. (This well-established fact is one reason why "believers" can select their data on the terms of trade. They simply select any period of falling prices and ignore the periods of rising prices.)

The reasons for this pattern are also well known. During a depression, when the demand for all goods falls off, manufacturers are able to restrict their production, and thus sustain their prices, more readily than farmers (who have a fixed amount of land) or mining companies (which have a heavy investment they want to keep in production). Conversely, during times of prosperity, manufacturers are better able to increase their production, so their prices do not rise so much. (Again, we refer to real prices.)

Wide fluctuations in primary prices harm consumers as well as producers, in both the first and the third worlds. Both producers and consumers must plan for months ahead, so they must estimate the prices on which they predicate their planning. Hence, it would be to everyone's advantage that prices be stabilized. The instruments of control are also well known, so why has it not happened? Before approaching this question, let us examine the instruments.

The control instruments are of two main types, one for commodities that can be stored and one for those that cannot. A mixture of these types can be used for commodities that can be stored for a period of time (say, two or three years) but will deteriorate thereafter.

For storable commodities, the instrument of control is the buffer stock. A fund is established for some commodity (say, tin); governments of importing countries contribute cash to the fund, and governments of exporting countries contribute the product (tin). All governments agree on ceiling and floor prices. If the price falls to the floor, the fund buys the product, and that added demand keeps the price from falling further. If the price rises to the ceiling, the fund sells the product, and the added supply keeps the price from rising further. The fund always makes a profit: It buys low and sells high.

Ceiling and floor prices must be set in such a way that the average price is unchanged; only the price variation is decreased. If the floor and/or the ceiling price is set too high, the fund will run out of money (and contain only the commodity), because it will buy earlier and sell later than it should. Conversely, if the floor and/or ceiling price is set too low, the fund will run out of commodity (and contain only money). We make one slight modification: Because the fund always makes a profit, it can buy a little more of the commodity than it sells, and thus it may create a slight upward bias in the average price. But this bias is probably negligible.

For nonstorable commodities, the instrument of control is restriction of production. Ceiling and floor prices must again be agreed upon, but this time the floor price is protected, not by buying the product, but by restricting its production. The managers of the agreement must predict what quantities will be necessary to keep the price at the floor or above, and governments of producing countries must allocate quotas among companies and individuals. If demand turns out to be greater than they had expected, and the market price approaches the ceiling, then they lift the quotas. The arrangement is imperfect in that by the time the demand is known, the crop may be already planted, and it is too late either to increase or to restrict it further.

Combinations of the two types of control have been used for crops such as coffee and sugar, for which both buffer stocks and restrictions have been applied.

Commodity agreements of both these types have been tried since the 1930s, but, except for OPEC, none has stood the test of time. A few recently negotiated agreements exist at any time (including the present), but except for them, all agreements have failed. Why?

We believe there are two principal reasons: disagreement between producing and consuming countries and disagreement among producing countries.

In virtually every commodity agreement so far negotiated, the producing countries have argued for as high a ceiling and floor as possible. This practice implies that those countries want to use the commodity agreement, not just to stabilize prices, but to increase the average price as well. Sometimes they cite the alleged decline in the terms of trade as their justification. At other times, they do not mention that problem, but "stability" becomes a euphemism for "increase." Governments of consuming countries, on the other hand, view themselves as the ultimate contributors to funds that run out of money. If by some chance an agreement is reached, some of the parties soon discover that it is not to their advantage, and they withdraw.

Disagreements among producing countries are usually over quotas. These disagreements occur not only when the compact is being negotiated, but also after it has been put into operation. Inevitably, some producers are more powerful than others—for example, it has often been said that Brazil dominates the coffee agreement. Countries that feel cheated by the quota assignments will not consider it a sin to "sell extra," under the table. If one country is "cheating," others will follow. Since no international tribunal exists to bring the offenders to book, the agreement lapses.

It is against this sorry background of experience that the South is calling for a super commodity agreement: the commodities fund.

The Commodities Fund

Since the terms of a commodities fund have not yet been negotiated, descriptions of it vary. But the proposal seems to be for an agreement that would encompass both types of instruments of control—buffer stocks and production restrictions—and all commodities. The major argument in favor of such a fund is that it would be economical. If a single cash fund would "stabilize" the prices of a number of commodities, then surplus cash from one commodity could be used to finance a deficit for another, and the total cash requirement would be reduced.

After much reluctance, governments of the industrialized countries have agreed in principle to a commodities fund. We suspect, however, that these governments may have been persuaded, not on the grounds of good economics, but by the political necessity of bringing the NOPECs to their side.

The justification for a super fund ought to be that earlier attempts failed because they were not large enough or were not all-encompassing. But it is difficult to see how a super agreement would solve the discords over quotas, price increases versus price stabilization, or selling under the table. Rather, these disagreements would be magnified, for failures with one or two commodities alone might be sufficient to bring down the whole structure.

The commodities fund proposal, therefore, contains all the hazards that have thwarted similar agreements for over half a century. But one more potential hazard is added. Suppose the fund acquires money by selling tin contributed by Bolivia, Malaysia, and other countries, and, at approximately the same time, it spends funds to buy copper produced by Chile, Zambia, and others. Clearly, the Bolivians and Malaysians will be subsidizing the Chileans and Zambians. Tin producers will have been forgoing price increases that the market might have provided them, and their money will be used to help copper producers whose prices might otherwise have fallen.

Indeed Behrman (1979) has shown that the UNCTAD proposals for a commodities fund imply a net subsidy by copper and tin producers to producers of the other "core commodities." We know of no instance in the past of third world countries' being so magnanimous toward each other, and we somehow doubt that they will be in the future. This fact alone might well cause the breakdown of the fund.

It is unfortunate that third world negotiators have been uncompro-
mising on the list of commodities to be included in the common fund.
Behrman (1979) has carefully surveyed the potential payoffs from price
stabilization and has demonstrated that not all commodities prices are
amenable to stabilization in the same way. Each commodity requires a
different amount of buffer stock to achieve a given degree of price
stabilization (depending upon elasticities of supply and demand). In
some cases, the carrying charges on the buffer stocks are so high that
they offset the gains to be expected from price stabilization. To include
those commodities weakens the case for a common fund.

Empirical work (such as Behrman's) can reveal the list of commodities
for which price stabilization yields net benefits. That list constitutes the
basis for an international price stabilization fund that might be agreed
upon by both third world and developed country participants. For those
commodities not included on the list, a scheme of compensatory finance
seems most appropriate (see Kreinin and Finger 1976).

Conclusion

The Declaration of a New International Economic Order calls for a
"just and equitable relationship" between the prices of primary products
and the prices of manufactured goods. Both the North-South dialogues
and the meetings of the United Nations Conference on Trade and
Development (UNCTAD) reveal that many third world diplomats believe
that the terms of trade for primary producers (prices of their exports
relative to those of their imports) tend to decline persistently over a
long period. They also appear to believe that third world countries are
the major exporters of primary products and importers of manufactured
goods from the industrialized world. In fact, neither of these premises
is correct.

The solution proposed for the terms of trade would be to index the
prices of primary products to those of manufactures and to enforce the
indexing by a commodities fund, which, by means of buffer stocks and
restrictions on production, would support prices.

But a solution to a problem that is not a problem will not work.
There is no tendency for the terms of trade to deteriorate for primary
products, and people who maintain that they do can substantiate their
belief only by selective perception: choosing commodities whose prices
have declined and ignoring those whose prices have risen, or choosing
time periods of decline and omitting periods of increase. Furthermore,
the industrialized countries export more primary products than does the
third world. For the most part, the production of primary products is
in the hands of the rich, either first world MNCs or private persons

or government companies in the third world. Poor people, on the other hand, are the consumers of the primary products or of the goods manufactured from them. Thus, legislated increases in primary-product prices would most likely transfer income from the poor to the rich, not the other way around.

Not only would indexing not transfer income from rich to poor, but it would create inefficiencies that, by increasing the costs to third world countries, would delay the development of those countries. The price of each product should depend on the cost, productivity, and demand conditions of that product. To force a product price to respond to conditions relating to a different product may cause the price of the first to be too high for all output to clear the market or too low to cover costs.

Advocates of NIEO, who normally criticize the monopolies of industrialized countries, propose to make cartelization, restriction of output, and higher prices ingredients of an international economic order. Are they not aware that, historically, the command of institutions changes hands over time? Hence, it becomes essential to select institutions that are equally appropriate no matter who is in charge—not institutions that are "right" when controlled by some people and "wrong" if controlled by others.

There are indeed efficient ways to transfer income from rich to poor: by taxing the former and either spending the proceeds on the latter or subsidizing them directly. If it is believed that these ways are not politically feasible, then it must be replied that the NIEO proposals are also not in line for quick acceptance. The North-South dialogues drag on. Although the North, in a political concession, now favors a commodity fund "in principle," the precise design of such a fund is as elusive as the ideal design for commodity agreements has been for half a century.

But conditions change over time, and ultimately, efficient arrangements are more likely to be accepted than inefficient ones. Therefore, since neither of the two policies appears politically feasible at the moment, we prefer to struggle for the one that makes greater economic sense.

Notes

1. This is not to say that scholarly work that focuses upon aspects of the terms of trade has not continued. Findlay (1980) presents an alternative theoretical argument why the terms of trade may deteriorate for the third world. His theory has not yet been tested empirically, and it relies on a set of very restrictive assumptions. Some of these, such as complete production specialization in the

North and South and no capital mobility between regions, would not stand up under empirical scrutiny. Krugman (1979) presents a model of trade and technology transfer based upon the so-called product cycle theory (see Chapter 3), which implies an improvement in the terms of trade for LDCs.

APPENDIX

Terms-of-Trade Indexes

"The belief" inevitably refers to the barter terms of trade, defined as follows:

$$\frac{P_x}{P_m}(100)$$

in which P_x is a price index for exports, and P_m a price index for imports.

But the barter terms of trade normally decline for a successfully developing society, since productivity increases enable it to sell for less to the rest of the world and it decreases its prices in order to obtain the business of other countries. Therefore, economists often prefer to judge a nation's progress by the income terms of trade (sometimes known as the single factoral terms of trade). Those are the ratio of factor earnings in the production of an export good to the prices of imports, or

$$\frac{F_x}{P_m}(100)$$

in which F_x may represent the earnings for an hour of labor, a unit of capital, or some other factor of production. A different index may be prepared for each factor, or some combined index may be used to represent all factors of production. Suppose an hour of labor earns \$1, and \$1 will buy a certain quantity of imports. The capacity of labor to buy imports then depends not only on P_m, but also on F_x, which, in turn, depends on both productivity and the price of exports. As the productivity of a factor of production increases, its capacity to command imports increases. We would argue that third world governments should be more concerned about the productivity of their factors of production than about the prices commanded by them. It is even possible that higher prices will cause a *decrease* in productivity, since they would allow inefficiencies to be tolerated—but that possibility, of course, is conjectural.

A third formula for terms of trade would compare F_x with F_m (factor earnings in the country from which imports are purchased). Known as the double-factoral terms of trade, this formula has little significance for the present analysis, for importers are not normally concerned with *why* prices are changing in exporting countries (whether for productivity or demand reasons). The double-factoral terms of trade would be useful in comparing the relative rates of economic development of two countries, however.

Complete discussions of the different kinds of terms-of-trade indexes are found in Viner (1937) and Meier (1968). Kindleberger's statement (1956, p. 236) that the terms of trade do not move against primary products in favor of manufactures is the relevant finding for a proposal to index. Kindleberger did, however, also find that when the terms of trade were unadjusted for quality, they ran against the less developed countries. Here, however, he distinguished between LDCs and producers of primary products, which are (as we have also pointed out) not identical. Kindleberger's hypothesis is that LDCs may not be able to transfer factors of production from a less profitable enterprise to a more profitable one as readily as MDCs. If this hypothesis is correct, then an increase in the prices of primary products would not be the appropriate policy response (and indexing even less so). Instead, LDCs should increase their institutional capabilities, information procedures, and similar facilities for factor mobility.

When adjustment was made for quality improvements in manufactured goods, Kindleberger found that the terms of trade moved heavily in *favor* of LDCs. By quality adjustments, he means that instead of counting the terms of trade of, say, automobiles for copper, one should count the services that each automobile or pound of copper would render: later-model automobiles that would last longer, go farther, or provide greater speed or improved fuel consumption should be considered as "more automobile" than earlier models. When such adjustments are taken into account, weighting becomes a subjective matter. Because people will disagree with the particular weights implied by Kindleberger, we believe that terms-of-trade analysis is futile.

Terms-of-Trade Theory

The classical theory of terms of trade, showing why these terms depreciate for innovating countries, was developed in the nineteenth century, principally by John Stuart Mill, Alfred Marshall, F. Y. Edgeworth, and F. D. Graham. The contributions of each are outlined in Viner (1937, pp. 535-55). Using reciprocal offer curves, Meier (1968, pp. 1-65) specifies the gains from trade by type of exchange.

Meier distinguishes between increases in factor availabilities and technological improvements as reasons for productivity changes. He also takes into account changes in consumer preferences. Each of these effects may be neutral (with respect to exportables and importables); export biased (if it causes a greater increase in production or consumption of exportables than of importables); import biased (if the other way around); ultra export biased (if the increase in exportables is so great as to draw factors away from importables, thus decreasing their production or consumption absolutely); or ultra import biased (if the other way around).

Meier modifies the classical theory by pointing out that a negative move in the terms of trade can be expected for neutral, import-biased, export-biased, or ultra-export-biased changes only (p. 47); ultra-import-biased changes would lead to improved terms of trade. As an example of the latter situation, suppose a cheap coffee substitute were discovered in the United States. Imports of coffee would decline (the substitute is treated as an importable), and factors of production that might otherwise produce exportables would be drawn away to produce the substitute. Presumably, the decline in the U.S. demand for foreign coffee would be greater than the decline in U.S. production of exports; hence, the U.S. currency might appreciate in the international market, and the terms of trade would improve for the United States.

We offer the above point as a theoretical qualification of the general statement on innovation and the terms of trade that we made in the text. Meier considered this case to be exceptional and certainly not representative of the bulk of changes in productive/consumption patterns in the industrialized world. Prebisch obviously did not base his case on ultra-import-biased innovations. We may thus presume that for the vast majority of innovations, the classical theory still holds.

Bibliography

Bairoch, Paul. *The Economic Development of the Third World Since 1900,* Chapter 6: "The Terms of Trade" (pp. 111–134). Berkeley: University of California Press, 1975.

Bauer, Peter T. *Dissent on Development.* London: Weidenfeld and Nicolson, 1971.

Behrman, J. R. "International Commodity Agreements: An Evaluation of the UNCTAD Integrated Commodity Programme." In *Policy Alternatives for a New International Economic Order,* edited by W. R. Cline, pp. 63-156. New York: Praeger, 1979.

Dale, Edwin L. "Idea of Growing Disparity in World Prices Disputed." *New York Times,* May 25, 1975.

Ellsworth, P. T. "The Terms of Trade Between Primary Producing and Industrial Countries." *Inter-American Economic Affairs* 10:1 (Summer 1956), 47–65.

Findlay, R. "The Terms of Trade and Equilibrium Growth in the World Economy." *American Economic Review* 70:3 (June 1980), 291–299.

International Monetary Fund (IMF). *International Financial Statistics Yearbook.* Washington, D.C., 1979.

_____. *Annual Report.* Washington, D.C., 1980.

Kindleberger, Charles P. *The Terms of Trade: A European Case Study.* Cambridge, Mass.: Technology Press (MIT) and Wiley, 1956.

Kreinin, M. E., and Finger, J. J. "A Critical Survey of the New International Economic Order." *Journal of World Trade Law* 10:6 (September–October 1976), 493–512.

Krugman, P. "A Model of Innovation, Technology Transfer, and the World Distribution of Income." *Journal of Political Economy* 87:2 (1979), 253–266.

League of Nations. *Industrialization and Foreign Trade.* Geneva, 1945.

Lewis, W. Arthur. "World Production, Prices, and Trade, 1870–1960." *Manchester School of Economic and Social Studies* 20:2 (1952), 105–138.

_____. "A Review of Economic Development." Richard T. Ely Lecture. *American*

Economic Review 55:2 (May 1965), 1–16. *Papers and Proceedings of the 77th Annual Meeting.*

Meier, Gerald. *The International Economics of Development.* New York: Harper & Row, 1968.

Nurkse, Ragnar. *Patterns of Trade and Development.* Oxford University Press, 1961.

Nyerere, Julius K. "The Economic Challenge: Dialogue or Confrontation?" *International Development Review* 18:1 (1976).

Pinto, Anibal, and Kñakal, Jan. *América Latina y el cambio en la economía mundial.* Lima: Instituto de Estudios Peruanos, 1973.

Powelson, John P. "The Terms of Trade Again." *Inter-American Economic Affairs* 23:4 (Spring 1970), 3–12.

Prebisch, Raul. "The Economic Development of Latin America and Its Principal Problems." *Economic Bulletin for Latin America* 7:1 (February 1962), 1–22.

Schlote, W. *Entwicklung und Struckturnwandlungen des englischen Aussenhandels von 1700 bis zur Gagenwart.* Jena, 1938. English translation by W. O. Henderson and W. H. Chaloner, *British Overseas Trade from 1700 to the 1930s.* Oxford University Press, 1962.

Spraos, J. "The Statistical Debate on the Net Barter Terms of Trade Between Primary Commodities and Manufactures." *Economic Journal* 90:357 (March 1980), 107–128.

United Nations. *Relative Prices of Exports and Imports of Underdeveloped Countries.* New York, 1949.

───── . *Declaration of the Establishment of a New International Economic Order.* UN Resolution 3201 (S-VI). May 1, 1974.

───── . *Charter of Economic Rights and Duties of States.* UN Resolution 3281 (XXIX). December 12, 1974.

United Nations, Economic Commission for Latin America (ECLA). *The Economic Development of Latin America and Its Principal Problems.* New York, 1950.

Viner, Jacob. *Studies in the Theory of International Trade.* New York: Harper Brothers, 1937.

3
Trade Reform and the Generalized System of Preferences

The NIEO plan has proposed (I, 3, x) "implementation, improvement, and enlargement of the Generalized System of Preferences for exports of agricultural primary commodities, manufactures and semi-manufactures from developing to developed countries and consideration of its extension to commodities, including those which are processed or semi-processed."

The Controversy: GSP or MFN?

Under the old economic order, the counterpart to the Generalized System of Preferences (GSP) is the most-favored-nation (MFN) policy. A regular extension of MFN has evolved out of international bargaining formalized by the reciprocal trade agreements of 1934, which turned the tide in the United States away from a history of high tariffs.

Under the reciprocal trade agreements, the United States offered to negotiate with other countries for mutual reductions in tariffs. For example, the United States might lower its duties on French wine if the French would lower their duties on, say, U.S. wheat. Since the nations had already agreed that tariffs should not be discriminatory, any U.S. reductions on French wine would also be accorded to Italian wine, Chilean wine, and wine from any other country. Likewise, French reductions on U.S. wheat would be extended to Canadian wheat, Argentine wheat, and wheat from any other country. The result of the extensions is the current MFN policy, which means that there will be *no* most-favored nation; all nations will be treated alike.

Why, then, would the French and Americans negotiate? They would do so only if France were the major supplier of wine to the United States, and the United States a major supplier of wheat to France. Thus, France and the United States would gain most from the arrangement, even though the benefits would be extended to all other countries as well.

In 1948, the industrial countries drew up the Havana Charter for an international trade organization to supervise a code of fair conduct that would take into account not only tariffs but quantitative restrictions, trade subsidies ("dumping"), state trading, and similar practices. However, the Havana Charter was never ratified. Instead, governments began to meet periodically for multilateral negotiations. A number of countries would assemble so that three-way, four-way, and even wider bargains could be struck. In each case, MFN would be extended to all contracting parties. These arrangements became known as the General Agreement on Tariffs and Trade (GATT). As a result of successive GATT meetings, U.S. tariffs are now among the lowest in history.

The LDCs have been divided on whether to join GATT. Some LDCs, like Mexico, have argued that GATT benefits mainly the MDCs; others, like Brazil, have joined.[1] However, LDCs frequently complain that the bargains that are struck are not to their advantage. At the conclusion of the Tokyo round of GATT negotiations in 1979, LDC governments boycotted the proceedings to protest their displeasure (but they signed the agreement).

Since MFN calls for equal treatment for all countries and the GSP, for preferences to the third world, the two policies are alternatives. But GATT does not outlaw GSP as it has always allowed exceptions to MFN for "regional arrangements," such as Britain's preference system with Commonwealth countries. Although GSP is a new wrinkle, no one has challenged it.

The GSP is now in effect to a limited extent. The European Economic Community (EEC) first implemented GSP in 1971, and Japan followed suit in the same year. The EEC then extended GSP to all former colonies through the Arusha and Lomé agreements (1973 and 1975), and the United States granted it to all LDCs in the Trade Act of 1974. But the United States will grant preferences only if the new imports do not damage U.S. producers. In principle, these imports may capture a greater share of expanding markets, but they will not be allowed to affect the existing markets of domestic producers.[2]

In order to assess GSP versus MFN, let us first evaluate the recent experience of LDCs in world trade. Are their exports increasing or not? Is their relative share of world trade increasing or not? After discussing those questions, we will consider GSP in greater detail: its limitations, its efficiency, and the likelihood of its extension. Then we will consider how LDCs have fared under GATT negotiations: Have they truly been discriminated against by MFN? Finally, we will consider the likely results of an expansion of GSP versus reliance on MFN. We will also present our own proposals for GSP.

The LDCs in World Trade

How the LDCs are faring under the old order may have much to do with whether a new order is necessary. If the LDCs volume and/or share of world trade is increasing, then it is perhaps better to let the old order continue to operate. Some people have suggested that their share is decreasing, but this analysis depends on two types of error.

The first error is that of selective perception. When all years are taken into account, it is clear that the LDC share in world trade (like the terms of trade) has its ups and downs and that much depends on the base year and ending year chosen. The high percentages in the later seventies were caused in large part by the increased prices of oil and other primary products, and indeed, the percentage fluctuations largely reflect those gyrations.

The second error is that of the "aggregate explanation." For non-oil-producing LDCs (NOPECs), the relative share of world trade did indeed decline from World War II until the mid-seventies (thereafter it increased). However, the decline occurred whether the terms of trade were declining or rising and, hence, was not caused by the terms of trade. If not the terms of trade, what was the cause?

The first step is to disaggregate the data—according to countries, product types, and years—to see if the component parts behaved differently—and indeed they did. Let us therefore go into a more detailed study of LDC exports to try to pinpoint the causes of the persistent decline in the NOPECs' relative share of world exports until the mid-seventies.

LDC Export Performance

Table 3.1 reveals that LDC exports have certainly not been stagnant. All LDCs, taken as a group, increased their exports (in 1977 dollars) from $48.8 billion in 1950 to $274.1 billion in 1978, a 6.4 percent annual rate of growth. But aggregate figures reveal neither the substantial differences among countries nor the major events of the period. The OPEC embargo of 1973, which was followed by an oil price increase, must surely be the major extraordinary event. Also, the table shows that some great differences appear among the country groupings, such as between rapidly growing LDCs and the least developed LDCs (LDLDCs).

Of special note is the abrupt but unsustained increase in the value of exports of the major petroleum exporters. The real rate of growth of 52.9 percent between 1970 and 1974 (mostly in 1973–1974) fell back

TABLE 3.1
LDC Export Performance, 1950-1978

	All LDCs	Major Petro Exporters	Non-Petro Exporting LDCs	Rapidly Growing LDC Exporters	Least Developed LDCs	Countries According to Per Capita Income, 1976		
						$800	$400-$800	Under $400
Export Earnings (in million $)								
1950	18.7	3.8	14.9	4.7	.9	10.9	2.7	5.1
in 1977$	48.8	9.9	38.9	12.3	2.3	28.4	7.0	13.3
1960	27.6	8.7	19.1	5.0	1.4	16.5	4.6	6.6
in 1977$	56.6	17.5	39.1	10.3	2.9	33.8	9.4	13.5
1970	56.1	19.0	37.1	10.8	2.2	35.4	10.6	10.1
in 1977$	86.9	29.5	57.5	16.7	3.4	54.9	16.4	15.7
1974	226.3	132.1	94.2	31.7	3.3	168.1	34.0	24.3
in 1977$	276.1	161.2	114.9	38.7	4.0	205.1	41.5	29.6
1975	211.8	119.6	92.2	31.0	3.2	156.6	31.7	23.4
in 1977$	235.1	132.8	102.3	34.4	3.6	173.8	35.2	26.0
1978	294.7	148.8	145.8	58.3	4.6	213.3	46.8	34.5
in 1977$	274.1	138.4	135.6	54.2	4.3	198.4	43.5	32.1
Real Rate of Growth								
1950 - 1960	1.5	5.9	0.1	-1.8	2.3	1.8	3.0	0.1
1960 - 1970	4.4	5.4	3.9	4.9	1.6	5.0	5.7	1.5
1970 - 1974	33.5	52.9	18.9	23.4	4.1	39.0	26.1	6.5
1975 - 1978	5.2	1.4	9.8	16.4	6.1	4.5	7.3	7.3
1970 - 1978	15.4	21.3	11.3	15.8	3.0	17.4	13.0	9.3

Source: UNCTAD Handbook of International Trade and Development Statistics, 1979, Tables 1, 3.

Notes: 1977 dollar figures are generated by applying the U.S. Implicit Price Deflator to the figures supplied by UNCTAD. "Major petroleum exporters" are defined as those countries for which petroleum and petroleum products accounted for more than 50% of their total exports in 1974. These countries are: Algeria, Angola, Bahrain, Brunei, Ecuador, Gabon, Indonesia, Iran, Iraq, Kuwait, Libyan Arab Jamahiriyah, Nigeria, Oman, Qatar, Saudi Arabia, Trinidad and Tobago, United Arab Emirates, and Venezuela.

"Rapidly growing LDC exporters" are countries whose exports of manufactures: (i) amounted to more than $800 million in 1976 and (ii) grew at an average annual rate of more than 20% during the period 1967 to 1976; they are Argentina, Brazil, Hong Kong, Republic of Korea, Mexico, and Singapore.

"Least developed countries" are: Afghanistan, Bangladesh, Benin, Bhutan, Botswana, Burundi, Cape Verde, Central African Republic, Chad, Comoros, Democratic Yemen, Ethiopia, Gambia, Haiti, Laos, Lesotho, Malawi, Maldives, Mali, Nepal, Niger, Rwanda, Samoa, Somalia, Sudan, Tanzania, Uganda, Upper Volta, Yemen Arab Republic.

Discrepancies in totals due to rounding.

to 1.4 percent for the period 1975–1978. Price increases of the magnitude set by OPEC must reduce consumption, and although price increases subsequent to 1974 have received much attention in the press, the equally newsworthy inflation rates of MDCs have taken their toll on OPEC's export proceeds.

Less spectacular, but more steady, rates of growth of exports among the NOPECs have had largely the same effect on the export levels of those countries. The 11.3 percent rate of growth in real terms for this group caused their exports to more than double in the years 1970–1978. The more rapidly growing LDCs' exports more than tripled during the same period, sustaining an annual growth rate in excess of 15 percent.

There is a sharp contrast between the export performance of the oil exporters and the other LDCs. Oil export revenues increased abruptly in 1974, but then they stagnated as the higher prices caused consumers to retrench. Other LDCs expanded exports at a much more steady pace and this has had much the same overall effect as oil price increases. In 1970, petroleum exporters accounted for 34 percent of total LDC exports; the 1974 price increases pushed that proportion to 58 percent. After 1974, however, the other LDCs took advantage of world markets and regained part of their previous position. By 1978, total LDC exports were roughly equally split between petroleum exporters and other LDCs. Indeed, the export revenues of oil exporters was 14 percent *below* 1974 levels in real terms, and those of other LDCs was 18 percent *above*.

The world recession (1974–1975) and stagnation (1975–present) have had their effects. Export growth for all major categories of LDCs declined greatly from 1974 to 1975 and then grew more slowly than in the pre-1974 period. Oil exporters fared relatively worse than the other groups after 1974, and by 1978, they still had not regained the revenue levels of 1974. Other LDCs suffered a dip in the 1974–1975 recession but quickly recovered.

The following lesson may be drawn: Cartel gains may be only transitory. Although they may have their intended effect in the short run, a steady growth via normal market transactions may prove as effective in raising export revenue,[3] and cartel members must continually act in a concerted fashion to maintain their gains, whereas those countries that have taken advantage of the normal markets can act independently. Furthermore, the market-oriented economies become more diversified and suffer less from world economic difficulties than do cartel members.

Table 3.1 also shows that the LDLDCs did not expand their exports at the same rate as the LDCs. During 1970–1978, their exports as a proportion of the total fell from almost 4 percent to less than 2 percent.

Trade in Manufactures

LDC exports of manufactured goods have surged in recent years. Table 3.2 shows them increasing annually by 26.4 percent during 1970–1975 and in excess of 14 percent during the decade of the 1960s. Nevertheless, the share of LDCs in world trade declined somewhat in the 1960s and increased only slightly in the 1970s. Even though the rate of increase in LDC manufactured exports was at a historical high, the same was true of MDC exports. The latter experienced extraordinary growth in the sixties and seventies for several reasons. First, postwar reconstruction in Europe was largely complete by the late 1950s. Second, the EEC, formed in 1958, increased intra-European trade. Third, Japan entered the MDC group as an aggressive exporter. Fourth, the three major rounds of tariff negotiations (Dillon, Kennedy, and Tokyo) reduced trade barriers to levels that had not been seen since before World War I.

In the LDCs, trade throughout the seventies was still dominated by primary products (even though these exports grew more slowly than manufactures). Nonfuel primary-product growth of only 4.8 percent in the sixties, combined with that category's great weight in the total, caused LDC nonfuel exports to grow more slowly than MDC nonfuel exports, despite a higher rate of growth for manufactured items.

In summary, Table 3.3 shows the share of LDCs in world trade by world area and major product group. The declining share of LDC exports (from 30.8 percent in 1950 to 17.8 percent in 1970) was due as much to rapidly expanding MDC exports as to sluggish LDC growth during the 1960s. During the 1970s, LDC primary exports continued to grow more slowly than the world average; thus, the LDC share of world primary exports continued to decline. This decline was more than offset by a very rapid growth in manufactured goods, which, despite their smaller weight in the total, drew up the LDCs' total share of world exports during the late 1970s.

Other changes have occurred in the export performance of major world areas. The share of Africa in world trade continues to decline, because of that continent's high number of LDLDCs. Latin America in 1950 was by far the richest of the LDC areas and thus a major exporter. Its relative position was not maintained, however, because the protectionist (import substitution) policies of the 1950s and 1960s priced Latin American exports (of both agricultural and manufactured goods) out of international markets. The decline and then rise in the Asian component hides relative shifts in trade participation among Asian countries. The major exporters in 1950 were in South Asia (e.g., India

TABLE 3.2
Value and Growth of Exports, 1960-1975

	Billion Dollars Value 1975	Average Annual Growth Rates (%) 1960 - 1970	Average Annual Growth Rates (%) 1970 - 1975
Developed Countries			
Total	578.0	10.1	20.9
Primary Products	118.0	6.6	18.0
Manufactures	421.9	11.4	21.2
Fuels	29.3	8.5	30.9
LDCs			
Total	210.0	7.2	30.7
Primary Products	53.0	4.8	14.5
Manufactures	31.3	14.4	26.4
Fuels	124.6	9.0	47.1

Source: United Nations, Monthly Bulletin of Statistics, various issues.

Note: Discrepancies in totals due to rounding.

TABLE 3.3
Shares of World Areas and Selected Commodity Groups in World Trade

	1950	1960	1970	1975	1978
Developed Market Economy Countries	61.1	66.8	71.5	66.1	67.4
Socialist Countries	8.1	11.7	10.7	9.7	9.7
Developing Countries	30.8	21.5	17.8	24.2	22.9
Latin America	12.4	7.9	5.5	5.4	4.9
Africa	5.1	4.1	4.0	4.0	3.5
Asia	13.1	9.5	8.2	14.6	14.3
Primary Commodities (excluding fuels)	n/a	36.1	30.5	29.0[a]	25.6[b]
Manufactures		3.9	5.4	6.3[a]	6.3[b]

Source: UNCTAD, Handbook of International Trade and Development Statistics, 1979, Table 1.9; and Yeats, 1979, p. 40.

[a] 1973

[b] estimate for 1980

Note: Discrepancies in totals due to rounding.

and Pakistan), where high-protection policies were followed. This group consistently failed to increase exports in comparison to East Asian countries such as South Korea and Taiwan, where import substitution was quickly converted to export promotion. Those countries, along with Hong Kong (which takes a free-trade stance), now lead the Asia group in export performance.

The transformation of LDCs into major exporters of manufactured goods is expected to continue into the near future. The World Bank study that is the basis for Table 3.4 projects that the LDC lead over MDCs in growth rates of manufactured exports will widen in the decade 1975–1985. Although growth rates continue to be very high for manufactured exports (Table 3.4 is in real terms), that of the LDCs is expected to be 12.2 percent compared to the modest 7.8 percent of the MDCs.[4] The transformation of LDCs from exporters of food and fuel to exporters of manufactured goods and fuel is illustrated by the proportional shift in the commodity composition shown in the last three columns. In terms of market growth, LDCs are expected to capture 13.6 percent of MDC imports in 1985, up from about 8.9 percent in 1975 (Chenery and Keesing 1979, p. 40).

Trade and the Newly Industrializing Countries

The acronym NICs (newly industrializing countries) has recently entered the jargon. Over the past decade or so, a few LDCs have increased their manufactured exports at very high rates. Table 3.5 shows the record of ten selected NICs, each of which had about $500 million or more in manufactured exports in 1976, amounting to about one-fifth or more of each country's total exports. Together these ten countries account for about 90 percent of LDC manufactured exports. If the weighted average growth rate, 24.4 percent, continues, these exports will approximately triple every five years.

The evolution of trade in the NICs reflects the product cycle described by Vernon (1966). These countries began their export manufacturing with highly standardized products such as textiles and yarn. As items first produced in the MDCs "matured,"[5] they began to be produced in LDCs (now the NICs), where producers found cost advantages in being able to use semiskilled, low-cost labor. Many of the NICs are now beginning to export capital goods, engineering products, and even automobiles. Also, as production becomes "internationalized," many NICs can economically produce standardized components for export. As increasing numbers of manufactured products mature and as the capabilities of the NICs improve, we can expect a greater production

TABLE 3.4
Past and Projected Rates of Export Growth by Product Group

	World 1960-75	LDCs 1960-75	World 1975-85	LDCs 1975-85	Percent of LDC Exports 1960	Percent of LDC Exports 1970	Percent of LDC Exports 1985
Fuel and Energy	6.3	6.2	3.6	3.4	39	40	30
Agricultural Products	4.2	2.6	4.4	2.1	32	27	20
Non-Fuel Minerals	3.9	4.8	4.2	5.8	7	7	7
Manufactures	8.9	12.3	7.8	12.2	11	26	43
TOTAL Merchandise	7.1	5.9	6.4	6.4	100	100	100

Source: Chenery and Keesing, 1979, p. 4.

TABLE 3.5
Exports of Manufactures of Selected LDCs

	Manufactures as % of Goods Exported		% of Absolute Poor, 1977	Manufactured Exports		
	1960	1975		Total 1976 (Million $)	Real Average Growth 1965-75	Income Per Capita 1976
Singapore	26	43	6	1790	15.0	2,700
Hong Kong	80	97	7	6480	11.9	2,110
Taiwan	14	81	<5	6921	28.8	1,070
Korea, Republic of	14	82	11	6675	36.0	670
Argentina	4	25	6	972	16.7	1,550
Brazil	3	27	8	2332	25.4	1,140
Mexico	12	52	10	2327	21.2	1,090
Turkey	25	36	11	466	32.2	990
Greece	9	48	<5	1252	28.7	2,590
Malaysia	6	18	9	667	18.2	860
Total for Group				29,882	24.4	

Source: Chenery and Keesing, 1979, p. 22. Percent of absolute poor is from OECD, Development Cooperation, 1979 Review, Paris: 1979, pp. 182-185.

of items that previously were considered "too capital-intensive" for LDCs.[6]

In a number of studies of LDC employment prospects, the International Labor Organization (ILO) has been urging governments to make a relative shift from import substitution to export promotion. Import substitution means producing those goods for which MDCs have comparative advantage (and LDCs have previously been importing)—hence, capital-intensive manufactures. Export promotion means encouraging the manufacturing of those goods for which LDCs have comparative advantage—hence, labor-intensive products. The NICs follow both policies, which essentially leads to the "intermediate technology" proposed by Schumacher (1974). In promoting exports, NICs have managed to reduce their proportion of absolute poverty to among the lowest for LDCs the world over. The percentages in Table 3.5, many less than 10 percent, compare with a whole range of percentages, almost all above 10 percent, many above 50 percent, and a few above 75 percent, in the remaining LDCs.[7]

Analysis of LDC Export Growth

Exports of manufactured goods from LDCs have increased phenomenally in the past decade. Despite record export growth among the MDCs, the LDCs have increased their growth rates even faster, raising the proportion of LDC manufactured exports enormously. This success has not been spread uniformly across all LDCs, however. Higher-income LDCs have increased exports most rapidly, and the exports of a number of those, the NICs, have grown spectacularly. The LDLDCs, still specializing in primary products, have not had the same success.

Why have manufactured exports done so well while exports of agricultural and other primary products have lagged? A major reason may be the subsidies of European agriculture set by the EEC's common agricultural policy, which limit Europe's ability to absorb agricultural imports. But poor performance can also be traced to LDC domestic policies. Chenery and Keesing (1979, p. 9), attribute it to an initial concentration on tropical products—such as coffee, cocoa, tea, and bananas—for which world demand has increased slowly. Also, LDC trade policies and tax systems, which are aimed at import substitution, have discriminated against agricultural production and exports. A major study sponsored by the National Bureau of Economic Research (summarized by Bhagwati 1978 and Krueger 1978) shows that foreign exchange rate systems associated with import substitution have been the main culprits in countries whose export performance has been poor (see also Little, Skitovsky, and Scott 1970). Even in spite of these self-imposed handicaps, agricultural output in LDCs has grown faster than it has in MDCs, but it has been "eaten up" by rapid population and income growths.

Manufactured exports have expanded most rapidly for those countries that rely on their natural comparative advantages. The list of NICs contains countries that have either always followed free-trade policies (Singapore and Hong Kong), have used import substitution to get industry started but quickly switched to export promotion (Taiwan and South Korea), or have abandoned import substitution when it became clear that exports and industrialization were being hindered by it (the remaining countries). The list of NICs in Table 3.5 contains no country that has stuck substantially to policies of exchange controls and import substitution. These countries have also learned to participate in a world trading system that has become increasingly liberalized, and in which trade among the MDCs has provided opportunities for the entire world trading community.

Trade analysts and policymakers make a big mistake when they concentrate mainly upon the *proportion* of LDC participation in various trade categories. For example,[8] the Second General Conference of UNIDO in 1974 set the goal of increasing the proportion of the world industrial output produced in LDCs to 25 percent by the year 2000 (currently, their share is 7 percent). However, if UNIDO's goal were to increase incomes and industrial output in LDCs, then the proportion becomes irrelevant.

LDC trade is directly affected by growth rates in MDCs. Indeed, when growth slackens in the MDCs, as it did in 1974–1975, trade opportunities for everyone are reduced.[9] Many opportunities for exporting to MDCs remain to be exploited (as the NICs are discovering), but doing so is easier when the MDCs are growing vigorously. But growth in both MDCs and LDCs may imply that their proportions of the total output, industrial and otherwise, may not change very much. Although it is likely that the LDC proportion of the world industrial output will expand, since their manufactured output and exports are currently growing at rates higher than in MDCs, any target expressed in proportional terms is not sensitive to the relationship between LDC industrial exports and MDC growth.

Limitations Imposed by the GSP

All the countries that now offer GSP place limitations on product coverage, money amounts, or countries included. Indeed, special treatments vary far more than one would expect from the word "generalized" in the title, and NIEO hopes to reduce the limitations. Coverage limitations include the following:

1. *Country limits.* Not all LDCs receive special treatment from each of the donor countries. OPEC, Spain, Portugal, and Greece receive no preferences from the United States. The EEC does not offer GSP to Malta or Taiwan, and the Japanese plan does not apply to certain exports from Hong Kong.
2. *Product limits.* Generally, products that compete directly with donor-country industry are excluded, especially industries for which the donor country may be losing its comparative advantage. The most important of these industries are textiles, clothing, and shoes, as well as some agricultural commodities in the EEC and Japanese programs.[10] Textiles and clothing are the main products of interest to the LDCs. Other items excluded are some fishery products, watches, and specialty steel items.
3. *Value limits.* Most donor countries place narrow limits on the value of imports qualifying for GSP treatment, and imports in excess of the amounts covered are subject to MFN tariff treatment. The EEC and Japan divide manufactured industrial items into product groups and place ceilings on the value of imports receiving preferential treatment from all beneficiaries combined. They specify that no more than 50 percent of any ceiling amount can be supplied by imports from a single LDC. The United States limits goods by applying a "competitive needs" rule. A beneficiary loses its preferential status for a specific product if its exports of that product to the United States exceed $25 million per year or account for more than 50 percent of all U.S. imports of the product.

The EEC limits on the amount of imports receiving GSP treatment from any one beneficiary were introduced with the justification that the limits would ensure an equitable sharing of benefits among the beneficiaries (UNCTAD 1975). Such a limitation would be reasonable if EEC imports were evenly spread across many LDCs. In practice, however, imports from beneficiaries are highly concentrated (Murray 1977). Experience has shown that once the principal beneficiaries have been excluded from further preference because they have reached their limits, other beneficiaries do not have the capacity to fill the remaining amounts allowed (UNCTAD 1977, p. 43).[11]

Special rules of origin may also limit coverage. These rules were introduced to guarantee that goods covered by GSP would be "substantially transformed" in the beneficiary countries, not just transshipped from nonbeneficiaries. For example, radios receiving GSP in the EEC must use transistors made in the beneficiary country. Since few LDCs can produce transistors, radios are therefore largely eliminated from GSP. U.S. rules require that preferential imports embody domestic processing costs and locally produced materials exceeding 35 percent of export value. This requirement eliminates some items with high indirect processing costs.[12] There is also a time limit on GSP programs. Most run for only ten years, and some GSP schemes will lapse after a shorter period of time. Given the protectionist mood in most MDCs, further extension may be doubtful.

UNCTAD (1979, p. 5) reports that only one-fourth of dutiable imports form LDCs (about $13.5 billion) are eligible for GSP. (Over half of LDC exports are already not dutiable in MDCs because they are primary products.) Even the $13.5 billion worth that are eligible do not all enter under GSP because some items have reached their value limits or are eliminated by rules of origin. Information from the EEC, the Scandinavian countries, and Japan indicate that only 54 percent of goods actually covered receive preferential treatment. In the United States, only about 18 percent of MFN-dutiable goods are covered by GSP.

Thus, the total effect of GSP is inconsequential. A $1,112-million export increase due to GSP is only 1 percent of the total exports of NOPECs, and because of a large number of exclusions, only 9 percent of the increase is in agricultural products. The largest share of the increases is in manufactures, and over half of those are due to preferences extended by the United States (Birnberg 1979, p. 236). Not all estimates are as high as Birnberg's. Hanson (1978, p. 258) cites studies finding that only $500 million of additional exports can be attributed to GSP yearly.

Most GSP benefits accrue to a short list of LDCs. Three-quarters of the trade increases in 1971 apply to only twelve countries (Baldwin and Murray 1977).[13] In 1974–1975 trade, U.S. preferences allocated 83 percent of the total benefits to ten countries,[14] three-fourths of the benefits going to countries with annual incomes above $700 per capita (Birnberg 1979, p. 224). UNCTAD (1979) reports that over half of the preferential EEC imports in 1974 came from only four beneficiaries (Yugoslavia, Brazil, Hong Kong, and India). These countries are already exporting their full quotas under GSP, so expansion would be subject to normal MFN tariffs. All twenty LDLDCs accounted for only 2 percent of the preferential imports of the EEC, Japan, and the United States.

Although the proportion of GSP benefits accruing to LDLDCs is small, the amounts may be large in absolute terms given the economic size of those countries. To them, the GSP may be very important in stimulating the export growth that has been so important to the NICs. Thus, one would not wish to reject the GSP outright simply because most of the benefits accrue to countries that apparently do not need the GSP to induce robust export growth.

Do MDCs Gain or Lose from the GSP?

In MDCs, the principal opposition to GSP arises, naturally enough, from producers whose products compete with the imported articles. Consumers, on the other hand, ought to favor it, for their prices would be reduced. There is, however, a third way to view GSP: Does a country as a whole gain?

A country as a whole would gain if its social costs were reduced— the social cost of a product is either its cost of production at home or the price paid abroad not including duty. A U.S. importer pays customs duties to the U.S. government—cost to the former, revenue to the latter, and therefore, zero social cost for the country as a whole. If a good can be produced in the United States for $1.00 or abroad for $.90, and if there is a duty of $.15, then consumers would have to pay more for the import, and the social cost to the United States is higher than it should be ($1.00 instead of $.90).

With GSP, the social cost would be reduced if (as in the case just cited) the reduction in duty causes Americans to buy abroad cheaper than they could buy at home. This result was dubbed "trade creation" by Viner (1950). But suppose Americans were already buying a product that costs $1.00 in Japan and paying a duty of 10 percent—consumers would pay $1.10, but the social cost would be $1.00—but because of GSP, the consumers could buy the same product from Brazil where it costs $1.05 (no duty because of GSP)? The social cost would increase from $1.00 to $1.05 (the nation as a whole is worse off by $.05). Viner (1950) called this situation "trade diversion" (buying from Brazil instead of Japan). Economists would say GSP is efficient if it results in more trade creation than trade diversion.

Trade creation and trade diversion due to GSP were estimated by Baldwin and Murray (1977) for 1971 and updated to 1974–1975 by Birnberg (1979, p. 236). Since the U.S. scheme did not go into effect until 1976, Birnberg applied the U.S. pattern of GSP preferences to the 1974–1975 trade. Total imports into the United States, the EEC, and Japan qualifying for GSP treatment in those years would have been $4,842 million, of which $1,112 million could have been attributed to GSP. Only $155 million of this increase (14 percent) would have been trade diversion; the remainder, trade creation. If this pattern continues, GSP is an efficient reform.

Generalized MFN Tariff Reductions

How well have LDCs fared under the GATT of the old economic order?

Three major rounds of GATT negotiations occurred in two decades: the Dillon round (1960–1961), the Kennedy round (1962–1967), and the Tokyo round (1973–1979). Most of the bargains were struck among MDCs, as they were the principal suppliers; LDCs were not principal suppliers of many products but they would benefit by extensions of MFN treatment to them (known as "MFN spillovers").

Over the three rounds of tariff negotiations, benefits to LDCs have continuously grown. In the Dillon round, 93 percent of LDC benefits came from spillovers (Finger 1974), which affected traditional exports only a little. But LDC nontraditional exports (similar to goods traded among MDCs) responded significantly to spillovers. Although small in absolute terms, they expanded (to the United States) more relatively than did MDC exports in the same categories.

A much larger benefit went to LDCs in the Kennedy round, again mostly from spillovers. The elasticities of supply (i.e., ease of increasing production) of eligible items were apparently greater for LDC exports to the United States and Japan than for MDC exports in the same categories (Finger 1976, p. 95).[15] The main difference between the Dillon and Kennedy rounds is that in the latter, the LDC exports affected were quite large ($2 billion in 1964). Unlike the Dillon round, both traditional and nontraditional LDC exports expanded after the Kennedy round at least as rapidly as MDC exports.

There has not yet been enough time to measure the results of the Tokyo round, which ended in 1979. They have been projected by Cline et al. (1978), using 1971 as a reference point, and those estimates have been updated to 1974 by Birnberg (1979). These authors applied proportional changes in import prices to measures of elasticity of supply in each country, assuming a 60 percent tariff cut across the board (the maximum allowed by the U.S. Trade Act of 1974). Eventual tariff cuts were on the order of 30 percent. Since Cline and Birnberg employed a linear estimation technique within product categories, we report their figures adjusted for the final 30 percent tariff reduction. Separate projections were made for hypothetical cuts in agricultural tariffs and nontariff barriers (NTBs), such as quota restrictions, and for textiles as opposed to the rest of manufacturing. Potential trade increases for the 1974 trade pattern (expressed in millions of $1980) added up to the following:

Agricultural goods (tariff reductions only)	$ 633
Manufactured goods (excluding textiles)	$1,124

Textiles $1,263
Agricultural goods (NTB reductions only) $ 340

The total of $3,360 million is about 2.2 percent of 1974 LDC exports. Slightly under half of that, however, is attributable to the two categories where trade liberalization is not likely to occur: textiles and agricultural NTBs.

However benefits are reckoned, they are concentrated among a relatively small number of countries. Hong Kong and Taiwan receive about 34 percent of the benefits if textiles are excluded; 41 percent including textiles. The top ten beneficiaries receive 75 percent excluding textiles; 67 percent with textiles.[16] There is also a notable concentration of benefits among upper-income LDCs (per capita income of $700–$2,000). Those LDCs have about 65 percent of the export increase, while countries with per capita incomes below $300 account for only 7 percent. In the former countries, export increases are on the order of $7.90 per capita; in the latter, $0.22 (Birnberg 1979, p. 224). The primary reason for this difference is that the lowest-income countries export mostly food and raw materials, which already face low or nonexistent tariffs. High-income LDCs devote a large portion of their productive capacities to manufacturing and can therefore take advantrage of tariff reductions.

Trade barrier reductions in the most difficult areas—textiles and agriculture—would benefit a few countries disproportionately. Reductions in agricultural NTBs would require reducing the variable levy on agricultural products in the EEC. A 60 percent reduction of agricultural NTBs in general would cause 90 percent of the LDC export expansion to flow to the EEC, and Argentina alone would account for 45 percent of that expansion. The same measure would augment the agricultural exports of the United States, Canada, Australia, and New Zealand by over $2 billion, most of it to the EEC. A 60 percent reduction in textile tariffs would have a greater overall effect than the same measure applied to other manufacturing categories, but 76 percent of the textile export expansion would occur in Hong Kong, Taiwan, and South Kórea. Birnberg (1979, p. 233) has pointed out that those three countries are beginning to play the role of principal suppliers of textiles and that MDCs are not likely to offer concessions on textiles until they provide some form of reciprocity.[17]

Erosion of GSP Benefits

LDCs have resisted across-the-board tariff reductions, which are mainly negotiated among MDCs, on the grounds that tariff preferences achieved within the GSP will be eroded through the reversal of trade diversion.

MFN tariff cuts would restore the competitive power of MDCs in the markets where GSP commodities are sold, turning purchases back to the original low-cost producer (presumably an MDC). However, the total amount of trade diversion is very small, only about 10 percent of the expansion of LDC exports attributed to the GSP. Furthermore, many of the goods covered by the GSP were not competitive with industries in the MDCs to begin with, which is no doubt why MDCs considered them for special treatment.

The erosion of GSP benefits by MFN tariff reductions has been exaggerated by some proponents of GSP. For example, UNCTAD (1980, p. 21) reasons that the loss from preference erosion due to the MFN tariff reductions of the Tokyo round is not offset by the gains due to the lower tariffs. But the method of analysis is faulty in that no account is taken of the limits associated with GSP, which are in effect removed by MFN treatment. Also, UNCTAD assumes (1980, p. 25) that trade creation from tariff reductions can take place only for goods not receiving GSP treatment. But that is not the case when goods receiving GSP treatment reach the quantitative limits. MFN tariff reductions on such goods surely shift purchases to low-cost suppliers (trade creation), and excluding this effect biases the conclusion in favor of net trade diversion. Indeed, the fact that some countries have reached a quantitative GSP limit must be taken as evidence that they are competitive in that product and that tariff reductions on goods beyond the limit will create trade that favors them.

Against GSP benefits, one must compare the benefits that flow from MFN tariff reductions—even if the latter occur through spillovers. GSP has the disadvantage of limited value and product coverage, which is not usually the case with MFN. Furthermore, the primary beneficiaries of GSP are now at their value limits, and further export expansion is subject to normal tariffs. Thus, the trade-expansion effect of MFN tariff reductions could be quite large.

Empirical work (Birnberg 1979, pp. 237–238) indicates that GSP erosion would amount to about $155 million (in 1980 dollars) compared to export expansion through MFN of $2,400 million—after adjustment for trade already created by GSP. Baldwin and Murray (1977, p. 44) have indicated that only if all value, product, and time limits were removed from GSP coverage would MFN benefits be less than those of GSP. But almost all authors indicate the extreme unlikelihood of this GSP extension. Furthermore, a basically unlimited GSP would surely cause sharp increases in trade diversion, since GSP extensions would begin to cover some goods for which there is LDC and MDC competition. Thus, as a reform, GSP would become increasingly inefficient compared to MFN tariff reductions.

Conclusion

LDC exports have expanded in recent years as never before. Despite the rapid export expansion of MDCs, LDCs have increased their share of world exports, and in many cases, manufactured goods have led this trend. It is expected that during the 1980s, the volume of manufactured exports from LDCs will continue to grow faster than that from MDCs.

Trade reforms have aided in LDC export growth. GSP has been an efficient reform, though quantitative limits have kept total benefits small in relation to overall LDC trade. MFN tariff reductions have had a much larger impact upon LDC exports, largely because the reductions do not have the same limitations as GSP. In either case (GSP or MFN), a small group of countries, the NICs, have benefited relatively more than other LDCs.

Exports from the NICs have expanded rapidly, even though neither GSP nor MFN has had an impact on them. Structural transformations in these countries allow them to compete effectively in the world trading community, and the primary benefits of expanding either the GSP or new MFN tariff reductions would accrue to the NICs. OECD (1979, pp. 36–37) has pointed out that NIC access to OECD markets under GSP has been very restricted, since most NICs quickly reach the quantitative limits. MDCs are reluctant to increase LDC preferences or otherwise liberalize trade further because the MDCs fear increased competition from the NICs.

The LDLDCs do not benefit much from either GSP or MFN. Most of the exports of these countries are primary products upon which MDCs do not levy tariffs to begin with, and their industrial bases are too weak to take advantage of the trade preferences for manufactured goods. The LDLDCs contrast sharply with the NICs, whose manufactured exports are likely to grow rapidly no matter what preferences are offered.

In the MDCs, current sentiment is toward greater trade restrictions, not less. Are we not therefore discussing a moot point when we make suggestions for reducing trade barriers for LDCs? We think not. Much of the reasoning behind the "new protectionism" (see Balassa 1980) is based on a fear that MDC labor-intensive industries are being threatened by a flood of imports from LDCs. That flood emanates primarily from the NICs. Since the NICs can compete in many of those industries with or without GSP,[18] proponents of greater protection see the GSP as unnecessary and in most cases "unfair."

Although we do not expect great trade liberalization in the 1980s, we believe that liberalization is more likely when the perceived costs to the MDCs are minimized. MFN trade barrier reductions are least costly since they imply reciprocity. GSP is perceived to be more costly since its benefits are extended largely to countries that do not need them (the NICs) and there is no reciprocity. As currently constituted, an expansion of GSP would imply that MDCs must bear the costs of nonreciprocal trade preferences for both NICs and LDLDCs, though it is only the latter group that may need GSP to stimulate export growth. The cost of extending GSP to the LDLDCs would be quite small if the same benefits did not have to be extended simultaneously to the NICs.

Future preference patterns should move toward integrating NICs with MDCs in MFN trade negotiations, and both NICs and MDCs should offer GSP to the LDLDCs. The NICs should be gradually phased out of the GSP and enter multilateral trade negotiations, as the MDCs do. Empirical studies show that NICs would benefit more from MFN tariff cuts than from GSP expansion and that some NICs are now beginning to play the role of principal suppliers (e.g., South Korea, Taiwan, and Hong Kong for textiles). Thus, they will be able to participate more fully in future MFN negotiations.

If NICs participated in GSP schemes for the exports of the LDLDCs, the latter would receive several new advantages. First, the MDCs would be more likely to be willing to expand GSP, since the fear of a flood of duty-free imports from NICs would be removed. Second, NICs should constitute a significant new market for manufactured goods from the LDLDCs. Many of the NICs are now investing in other LDCs with an eye toward obtaining cheaply manufactured components, which they in turn assemble into the export items destined for MDC markets. Third, although a GSP for LDLDCs only is not likely to spur manufactured goods from industries that do not yet exist, it would create a more favorable environment for those countries when they do create an industrial base. As LDLDCs invested in new industry, fewer obstacles to export expansion would exist.

Participation in reciprocal trade barrier reductions with MDCs also implies a number of benefits for the NICs. Since many of the goods that they export exceed the limits for GSP coverage, the true limits on their export performance are the barriers encountered on the open market. These barriers would become the object of reciprocal trade barrier reduction. In offering reciprocal tariff cuts, the NICs will have to open their economies to goods from the MDCs. Economic theory and empirical evidence support the view that benefits accrue to countries that open up their own markets in the form of improved competition, production efficiency, and lower prices to consumers (see Krueger 1978 and Little, Skitovsky, and Scott 1970).

The system of preferences should therefore be managed dynamically, with LDCs moving (through the NIC stage) into the MDC category and extending the benefits downward. This plan is not what the NIEO advocates have in mind. Their preference would be to expand the GSP—increase its commodity and value coverages—from the countries now granting preferences to the countries now receiving them.

Probably the strongest argument for *not* expanding the GSP is that LDCs must further increase the efficiency of their manufacturing industries if they are to expand their exports. We have shown that they have indeed expanded their exports under MFN—the old economic order—and that they are very likely to continue to do so (the increase is registered both in absolute amounts and in relative share of world markets). But most of their advantages have been via spillovers. In the future, more must be by direct bargaining. Only by lowering their *own* tariffs (through nonpreferential bargaining) can the LDCs further improve their efficiency as manufacturers.

Notes

1. For a list of members of the GATT, see A. S. Banks and W. Overstreet, *Political Handbook of the World, 1980* (New York: McGraw-Hill, 1980), pp. 635–637.

2. In an earlier work (Loehr and Powelson 1981, pp. 309–311), we go into more detail on the history of GSP.

3. Compare two countries with the same export revenue in year one. If one is able to double the revenue in year two but stagnates thereafter, it is no better off in year five than the second country, if the latter can increase exports at 15 percent per year.

4. One should recall that at 12 percent compounded per annum, the absolute increase in LDC exports would be 216 percent over the decade.

5. A mature product is one for which both the product and production technology have become standardized. Production in the mature stage no longer requires the judgment of highly skilled workers, as production in early stages does. Markets for mature products are also well developed.

6. For a good survey of the impact of MDC trade with the NICs, see OECD (1979).

7. Export promotion should not be construed as the sole force leading to such low percentages of absolute poverty. These same countries have promoted appropriate technology and income redistribution in other ways, such as by agrarian reform and decentralized decision making. We believe, however, that it is no coincidence that a number of countries that have adopted a similar set of policies (including export promotion) have been successful in reducing absolute poverty spectacularly.

8. Reported by Yeats (1979, pp. 41–46).

9. The trade of the LDCs was not affected as much as trade among the MDCs. The relative gap in export growth rates between MDCs and LDCs

widened in the late seventies. Both slowed their export expansion, but the MDCs slowed more.

10. The EEC offers limited coverage for textiles and clothing, if the exporting country abides by the restrictions of the Multifiber Arrangement.

11. Details on the proportions of overall quotas filled by countries that have reached their limits, by commodity group for the EEC, can be found in UNCTAD (1977).

12. This requirement may eliminate preferences for countries with very primitive industries, which begin by assembling components produced abroad. Many LDLDCs may have few industries with 35 percent domestic processing and materials costs.

13. Taiwan (excluded by the EEC), Mexico, Yugoslavia, South Korea, Hong Kong (partially excluded by Japan), Brazil, Singapore, India, Peru, Chile, Argentina, and Iran (excluded by the United States).

14. Mexico, Taiwan, Hong Kong, South Korea, Brazil, Israel, Singapore, Malaysia, India, and the Philippines.

15. The difference may not be of statistical significance.

16. Hong Kong, Taiwan, South Korea, Argentina, Mexico, Brazil, Israel, India, the Philippines, and Singapore.

17. Tariff reductions on textiles may not expand trade in any event, because of the nontariff barriers inherent in the Long Term Arrangement Regarding International Trade in Cotton Textiles (1962) and the Multifiber Arrangement (1974).

18. Recall that once NICs reach the quantitative limit imposed by GSP, they then compete, on the margin, as if the GSP did not exist.

Bibliography

Balassa, B. "The Tokyo Round and the Developing Countries." *Journal of World Trade Law* 4:2 (March–April 1980), 93–118.

Baldwin, R. E., and Murray, T. "MFN Tariff Reductions and LDC Benefits Under GSP. *Economic Journal* 87:345 (March 1977), 30–46.

Bhagwati, J. N. *Anatomy and Consequences of Exchange Control Regimes.* Cambridge, Mass.: Ballinger Publishing Co. for National Bureau of Economic Research, 1978.

Birnberg, T. B. "Trade Reform Options: Economic Effects on Developing and Developed Countries." In *Policy Alternatives for a New International Economic Order,* edited by W. R. Cline, pp. 217–283. New York: Praeger, 1979.

Chenery, H. B., and Keesing, D. "The Changing Composition of Developing Country Exports." World Bank Staff Working Paper. Washington, D.C.: World Bank, 1979.

Cline, W. R., et al. *Trade Negotiation in the Tokyo Round.* Washington, D.C.: Brookings Institution, 1978.

European Communities, Commission. "APC-EEC Convention of Lomé." *Courier* (Brussels), no. 31 (1975).

Finger, J. M. "GATT Tariff Concessions and the Exports of Developing Countries." *Economic Journal* 84:335 (September 1974), 566–575.

_____ . "Effects of the Kennedy Round Tariff Concessions on the Exports of Developing Countries." *Economic Journal* 86:341 (March 1976), 87–95.

Golt, S. "Special or Free and Secure Access to Markets for Developing Countries?" *World Economy* 1:1 (October 1977), 55–67.

Hanson, D. "Trade, the Developing Countries, and North-South Relations." In Adams, W., et al., *Tariffs, Quotas, and Trade: The Politics of Protectionism*, pp. 247–268. San Francisco: Institute for Contemporary Studies, 1978.

International Monetary Fund. *International Financial Statistics Yearbook*. Washington, D.C., 1980.

Kenya, Republic of. *Economic Development Plan, 1974–1979*. Nairobi: Government Printing Office, 1974.

Krueger, A. O. *Foreign Trade Regimes and Economic Development: Liberalization Attempts and Consequences*. Cambridge, Mass.: Ballinger Publishing Co. for National Bureau of Economic Research, 1978.

Little, I.M.D.; Skitovsky, I.; and Scott, M. *Industry and Trade in Some Developing Countries*. London: Oxford University Press, 1970.

Loehr, W., and Powelson, J. P. *The Economics of Development and Distribution*. New York: Harcourt, Brace, Jovanovich, 1981.

Murray, T. "Tariff Preferences and Multinational Firm Exports from Developing Countries." In *Issues and Prospects for the NIEO*, edited by W. G. Tyler, pp. 129–147. Lexington, Mass.: Lexington Books, 1977.

Organization for Economic Cooperation and Development (OECD). *The Impact of the Newly Industrializing Countries on Production and Trade in Manufactures*. Paris, 1979.

Schumacher, E. F. *Small Is Beautiful*. New York: Harper & Row, 1974.

Strange, S. "The Management of Surplus Capacity; or How Does Theory Stand Up to Protectionism 1970s Style?" *International Organization* 33:3 (Summer 1979), 303–304.

United Nations Conference on Trade and Development (UNCTAD). *Operation and Effects of the Scheme of Generalized Preferences of the European Economic Community*. TD/B/C.5/34. New York, July 1975.

_____ . *The EEC Scheme for 1976 and 1977*. TD/B/C.5/48. New York, March 1977.

_____ . *Operation and Effects of the Generalized System of Preferences*. New York, 1979.

_____ . *Assessment of the Results of the Multilateral Trade Negotiations: Implications of the Tokyo Round for the Trade of Developing Countries*. TD/B/778/Add. 1. New York, February 26, 1980.

United States. *International Economic Report of the President*. Washington, D.C.: Government Printing Office, 1975.

United States, Department of State. *Multinational Trade Negotiations*. Current Policy Statement, no. 56. Bureau of Public Affairs, Office of Public Communication. Washington, D.C., 1979.

Vernon, R. "International Investment and International Trade in the Product Cycle." *Quarterly Journal of Economics* 80:2 (May 1966), 190–207.

Viner, Jacob. *Studies in the Theory of International Trade*. New York: Harper Brothers, 1937.

———. *The Customs Union Issue*. New York: Carnegie Endowment for International Peace, 1950.

Yeats, A. J. *Trade Barriers Facing Developing Countries*. New York: St. Martin's Press, 1979.

4

Multinational Corporations

Diverging Philosophies

If NIEO advocates believe in any idea more tenaciously than the one about terms of trade, it is the one about multinational corporations (MNCs). Probably the most popular exposition of this idea occurs in *Global Reach*, by Barnet and Müller (1974), which speaks (p. 13) of MNCs in the same breath as Alexander the Great, the Napoleonic system, Hitler's Thousand-Year Reich, the British Empire, and Pax Americana. When we refer to "the belief" in the present chapter, we are referring to the idea that MNCs possess enormous financial and economic power, which they intend to use to command world trade and production to their own wealth and advantage, and that LDCs are their primary prey.

Our own philosophy is somewhat different: MNCs are indeed powerful, though not nearly so much so as "the belief" would imply, and there are controls to curb that power. We would prefer to see both the controls and the power dispersed through widespread stockholdings or cooperative ownership rather than concentrated in governments. LDC governments are not weak prey. They already possess a substantial arsenal of controls, which—we plan to show—harm the poor of their countries more than they help. We believe that to supplement that arsenal with the management of MNC assets would tilt power in the wrong direction.

We sense a historical contrast between MDCs and LDCs. MDCs have experienced three stages of governmental power, the LDCs only one. In the first MDC stage, the medieval economy was heavily controlled, first by kings and princes and later by the bourgeoisie and trading guilds, so that everyone except the controllers was largely unfree. Every facet of economic life was ruled by some higher authority: what would be produced and by whom, who would work for whom and at what wage, who was allowed to sell in which place and at what price.

"Enlightened" despots felt that they alone knew how to organize a society; they loved their poor but despised that group's abilities.

In the sixteenth century, there began to be gradual emancipation of the working classes from the authority of their patrons, and the second stage—that of liberalism—reached its apogee in the nineteenth century. By that time, the poor had exerted their leverage sufficiently to wring out such reforms as the end of serfdom, increased suffrage, universal primary education, shorter workdays, and labor unions. In the twentieth century, they obtained social security, unemployment insurance, health benefits, and other social legislation.

The third stage is again one of increased central control, but this time the purpose is to offset the excesses of private power concentrations (as through monopoly regulation), to provide the social benefits just mentioned, and to assure full employment and political rights. But each time the government has been vested with additional controls, some kind of safeguard has been set up—through parliamentary democracy, court reviews, rights of local and state governments, or even bureaucracy. These safeguards do not work perfectly, but they do work.

In their zest for centralized planning, however, we believe that international advisers and NIEO advocates may confuse the first stage in the LDCs with the third stage in the MDCs. In believing that a central government is indeed the protector of the poor, those advisers and advocates help endow it with capital, planning instruments, and patronage, which increase the already great imbalances of wealth, income, and power.

With NIEO, we face a quandary. We are not overly fond of MNCs, whose claims that they benefit the poor have surely been exaggerated. But we do see them as a countervailing power to national governments. The NIEO plan does not seek international controls over MNCs. Instead, it asks for "an international code of conduct" that (we surmise from the discussions that have occurred) would be enforced at the pleasure of national governments. But to ask the South African government, for instance, to regulate MNC "collaboration with racist regimes" is, of course, again like asking the fox to tend the chicken coop. As we shall see later in this chapter, the simile does not apply only to South Africa.

As we take up sixteen major complaints against MNCs, we will find that most problems have either been exaggerated or are already able to be controlled by LDC governments. Some criticisms are not well founded, but a few others are quite true and intractable. However, in no case will we discover that enhancing the power of governments is likely to mitigate the wrongs; indeed, it is more likely to introduce still new dilemmas.

Complaints Against MNCs

1. They Roam the World at Will

Barnet and Müller (1974) suggest that the power of MNCs lies in their "global reach." If they are not content with the regulations of one country, they can pack up and go to another. If wages or taxes are too high, MNCs can move to a country where those costs are lower. Since MNCs can move but countries cannot, the MNCs always have the advantage. In bargaining for terms, governments always lose.

Although attractive to many people, this assessment is hardly realistic. First, extractive companies are tied to the location of their mines or wells. If a petroleum company does not like the wages and taxes in Ecuador, it would accomplish little by moving to Uruguay—or even to Venezuela, where petroleum is nationalized. Manufacturing companies usually settle in LDCs to sell in the local market. A subsidiary in Mexico could not maintain its sales in that country if it moved to Guatemala. Furthermore, once a company has invested in land, buildings, and equipment, it cannot readily ship its plant abroad. The MNCs' mobility has clearly been exaggerated.

If MNCs had the supreme bargaining advantage, one would hardly have expected the extent and severity of controls that have already been placed upon them. Petroleum, copper, tin, and other mineral subsidiaries have been nationalized virtually throughout the third world, and even before nationalization, those products were subject to taxes that were often as high as 70 percent of gross profits. Manufacturing subsidiaries are restricted in most LDCs as to imports, prices, wages, and repatriation of profits. An examination of the record hardly reveals that governments are weak in bargaining power or too unsophisticated to exercise it.

2. They Are Sophisticated, Knowledgeable Negotiators

It is argued that even if MNCs are not so mobile as one might think, their knowledge of world conditions, their rapid communications, their computers, and the sophistication of their officers mean they always have the bargaining edge on LDC government officials.

The curious point about this complaint is that it is usually made in general, and when it is supported by specific examples, the incidents happened many decades ago. Juan Vicente Gomez, the dictator of Venezuela from 1908 to 1935, allowed the foreign oil companies to write their own laws, and he and the companies both profited. Similar examples are legion, particularly in regard to U.S. investments in Latin America. But Latin American governments are no longer run by undereducated dictators, and the few countries in Africa that are, are not the primary focus of U.S. investment.

We do not question the fact that corrupt government officials grant concessions to MNCs and "share the loot," and if the NIEO plan called for international controls to prevent this situation, we might be in favor of it. Instead, it calls for greater controls to be exercised by the same (sometimes corrupt) officials.

The governments of LDCs are rapidly increasing their own sophistication, knowledge, and communications. To the extent that disparities in capabilities are a problem, that problem is solving itself.

3. Their Wages Are Too High—Their Wages Are Too Low

Curiously, critics of MNCs argue both that their wages are too high and that they are too low. Sometimes the same critics voice both arguments in the same book. On page 170, Barnet and Müller (1974) criticize MNCs for paying higher wages than the local average, which gives them "every incentive to buy more machines and to employ fewer workers." On page 312, the same authors complain that MNCs pay lower wages in LDCs than they do in their home countries. "Should not the wages in Detroit and Hong Kong be the same?" they ask. Let us consider the two complaints separately.

Their Wages Are Too High. After witnessing many years of controversy, the International Labor Organization launched an investigation of wages paid by MNCs all over the world. Its findings (ILO 1976, pp. 49–50) were that for the most part, MNCs pay 50 percent higher wages than do national companies and that in LDCs, the average MNC wage is approximately 100 percent higher than the average. MNCs also provide more extensive benefits, such as housing, education, and health insurance.

Such practices, MNC critics argue, create a labor elite that is limited to a small proportion of the working force and enjoys benefits that are substantially better than those received by the bulk of the country's workers. Furthermore, in cases where machines may be substituted for labor, high wages encourage the firm to do so. Consequently, the wage policy of MNCs is not designed to alleviate the unemployment that exists in most LDCs.

We concur with the critics, but we ask further, Why do MNCs pay higher-than-market wages? One answer is that their greater efficiency (which is higher than that of national firms) enables them to do so and that by doing so, they can skim off the cream of the labor crop. Often their operations require disciplined labor (arriving on time, working full hours, working efficiently), and discipline is more likely if the worker receives privileges he doesn't want to lose. But a second reason lies in labor-union policy. In many LDCs, the unions are themselves elitist (restricting entry) and consider MNCs to be fair game (for higher wages are believed to reduce profits that would otherwise be taken from the country). In most LDCs, unions are protected by the Ministry of Labor, which helps negotiate their preferred status. High wages are often legislated, or agreed upon, as part of the package arrangements that permit the MNCs to function in the host country. (This situation again belies the image of the all-powerful MNC!)

The cost of high wages is high unemployment. Since workers without jobs are a blight on LDCs, we would prefer that the MNCs pay lower wages and hire more workers. We do not begrudge a firm's rewarding high-quality labor, but aside from that factor, the wage margin might well be reduced.

Their Wages Are Too Low. MNCs are also faulted for paying wages that are lower than what they pay for corresponding work in their home countries. Some people would suggest that if an MNC produces the same good, with the same technology, in the United States as in India, then if it earns a profit at all in the United States, it must earn an enormous profit in India.

Although we have never seen this argument researched, we suspect it does not stand muster. The assumption that either the same good is produced or the same technology is used in India as in the United States is hard to accept. Indeed, we have just seen that lower wages are a requisite for MNCs' hiring workers instead of machines, so it is unlikely that many MNCs would use similar technology in LDCs and MDCs.

In general, wages are determined by the productivity of the labor in a region, to which the labor productivity in a given plant conforms. Labor productivity (and hence, wages) may be low because a region lacks capital, technology, or labor skills, or for a host of other reasons. Firms normally accept the wage established by the local conditions. They hire more laborers and use less machinery, which causes the marginal productivity of labor to decline (as dictated by the law of diminishing marginal productivity) to that of the local market. To do otherwise would be to foment unemployment and create inequities. Surely, the wages in Hong Kong should not be determined by labor productivity in Detroit!

Our judgment is that MNCs probably pay wages that are too high (and therefore cannot also pay wages that are too low) but that correction of this problem is surely well within the capabilities of any LDC government. Most LDC governments choose not to correct it, and therefore, they surely would not do so if somehow they achieved greater control over MNCs through NIEO.

4. Their Profits Are Too High

What about the profits earned by MNCs in LDCs? Are those profits too high? That, of course, is a matter of opinion, but at least we can find out what the profits are. In the Appendix tables for this chapter, we have assembled data prepared by the U.S. Department of Commerce on direct investment (that department's term for U.S. investment abroad that is controlled by a parent company at home).

We immediately see that the profits of petroleum companies are very high. In 1978, profits were 82 percent of those companies' total investment, and in 1979, they were 107 percent (see Table 4A.3). In a single year, therefore, the companies earned back more than their investment. Hark back to Chapter 2 and let the lesson not be lost: If we were talking about copper, rubber, timber, coffee, or any of the commodities whose prices would be supported under NIEO, the principal gainers would be the multinationals, along with a few people in the LDCs who are already rich.

There is one qualification. Oil company investment made years ago is probably valued at earlier-year prices. Suppose, for example, a company invested $1,000 in 1970 and earned a profit of $200. We would say its profit was 20 percent on investment. Suppose all prices doubled by 1980, but otherwise nothing changed. The value of that investment becomes $2,000, and the profits $400. The rate is still 20 percent. But if the investment is kept on the books at 1970 prices ($1,000), and the profits are recorded at 1980 prices ($400), then the *nominal* return becomes 40 percent. Unless corporations adjust the book value of the earlier investment upward with inflation (and almost all do not), *real* profit rates are the nominal rates discounted for inflation. But even if we discount the oil companies' nominal rate by half to allow for inflation, the real rate is still very high.

But the same situation does not occur for other investments. The return on manufacturing has been creeping upward, from about 10 percent in the mid-sixties to 15 percent at the end of the seventies. We suspect the inflation illusion, and we would guess that real returns have not changed much. In the neighborhood of 10 percent, they are no greater than alternative investment opportunities at home. Indeed, if manufacturing MNCs should sell all their plants and equipment and put the proceeds in savings and loan accounts at current rates, they would probably increase their profits!

Curiously, U.S. investment in LDC petroleum, mining, and smelting operations (the high earners) increased but slowly during the sixties and seventies, but investment in manufacturing in LDCs jumped ahead by leaps and bounds. With the rash of nationalizations, the petroleum investment position declined from $5,051 million in 1966 to virtually zero in 1974; then it picked up again and reached $7,321 million in 1979 (see Table 4A.1). Thus in 1979, its nominal value was about 50 percent higher than in 1966; adjusted for inflation, it might have been about the same as or less than in 1966. Mining and smelting investments increased steadily from $1,655 million in 1966 to $2,267 million in 1972 (USDC 1979), declined to $1,784 million in 1974, and then went up to $2,416 million in 1979 (Whichard 1980) for a net nominal increase of 46 percent over the whole period. But the manufacturing investment position has steadily increased from $3,525 million in 1966 to $16,198 million in 1979. Starting from a much smaller base, manufacturing therefore increased its nominal investment by 360 percent, and it now outranks (in total amount) petroleum, mining, and smelting investments combined!

Why does the low earner steadily increase while the high earners oscillate? No one knows for sure, but we suggest the following explanation. Because of nationalizations, MNCs have been reluctant to invest in extractive industries in LDCs. Most such investments have therefore been specifically invited, with certain guarantees, to complement the production of national companies. Furthermore, LDC nationals feel quite capable of managing their extractive enterprises. In the case of manufacturing, however, they see some advantage in having well-known brand names produced in their countries. Thus, all automobiles sold in Mexico are produced there, by subsidiaries of MNCs, but bear the same brand names as if they had been produced in Germany, Japan, or the United States. We also suspect that LDC government officials believe the technology for manufacturing is more varied and more complex than for the extractive industries. Perhaps they feel less threatened by manufacturing, and therefore they have not nationalized it to the same degree and do not plan to do so soon.

Why do manufacturing MNCs consent to invest in LDCs? Surely not for profits. Again we suggest that perhaps they wish to have a global presence so that their brand names are known the world over. Perhaps there will be future opportunities that the manufacturing MNCs can benefit from only if they are already there. We believe the explanation must lie somewhere along these lines. Whether these reasons are good or evil is in the mind of the observer.

5. *They Do Not Reinvest Their Earnings*

In the United States, the bulk of business investment is internally generated by corporations: It comes from the excess of cash taken in over cash taken out. Sometimes this excess is called "depreciation allowances," and sometimes "undistributed profits." Because of generous tax laws on what may be deducted for depreciation, we suspect that depreciation allowances are overstated in the United States and undis-tributed profits are understated. But taken together, they far outrank personal saving as a source of investable funds.

Government officials of LDCs have somehow felt that in a similar vein, MNCs ought to reinvest their internally generated funds in the host countries rather than send them home. Unfortunately, we cannot tell to what extent MNCs really do reinvest earnings, for information on depreciation allowances is scanty. But we do have data on the portion labeled "profits." Whereas in the United States, corporations tend to distribute only about 40 percent of their profits as dividends (more or less in different years) and reinvest the other 60 percent, MNCs in LDCs have tended to transmit 75 or 80 percent of their earnings to the parent companies at home instead of reinvesting those earnings in the host countries.

Once again, however, the overall statistics are deceiving, and when we disaggregate them, a new picture emerges (see Table 4A.2). It is mainly in the extractive industries that repatriated earnings greatly exceed reinvestments. In manufacturing, there was no consistent pattern in the mid-sixties (in some years repatriated earnings would exceed reinvest-ments, and in some years not). Beginning in 1968, however, manufacturing companies increasingly reinvested their earnings in host countries, so that in 1978 they reinvested 65 percent, and in 1979, 56 percent (Whichard 1980). In short, their ratio abroad was approximately what it was at home.

The reasons for the difference probably have to do with the degree of welcome. It is possible that the extractive industries do not reinvest the bulk of their earnings for the same reason they are reluctant to make new investments: fear of expropriation. The manufacturing in-dustries probably reinvest for the same reason that they make new investments: to keep up their global presence.

In view of the record on profit making and profit reinvesting, what kinds of controls should NIEO impose? It would seem that such controls are most needed for petroleum investments, yet this is the one area in which host governments are already in control. They have nationalized the companies, determined the amounts to be produced, dictated the price, and taken most of the profits for themselves. What additional controls might NIEO offer? In manufacturing, on the other hand, the current trends are healthy: Profits are low, and reinvestments are in-creasing. We do not see in what ways NIEO controls would improve the behavior of manufacturing MNCs with respect to reinvestment of their profits.

6. *Their Profits Exceed Their New Investments*

It is often charged that MNCs "decapitalize" their host countries in two ways. First, each year they take out more in profits than they put in as investment (Vernon 1971, p. 172). Second, they borrow locally so that in fact, the host country supplies them with more capital than they themselves bring in. We analyze the first of these charges in the present section and the second in the next.

In 1979, MNCs invested $3.7 billion in LDCs and repatriated profits of almost $9.2 billion (see Table 4A.4). In 1978, investments were only about $2.9 billion compared to repatriated profits of $6.1 billion. A glance at the whole table shows only one year (1975) during the period 1966 to 1979 in which investments exceeded repatriated profits, and then by a paltry $133 million.

On the surface, the decapitalization argument appears proved. In fact, however, the surface appearance hides two distinct processes, and they must be considered separately. One relates to return on investment, and the other to the balance of payments.

Return on Investment. Suppose an individual deposits $100 in a savings bank on January 1 at 10 percent interest to be paid on December 31. At the end of of the year, he withdraws $10 in interest. On the next day (January 1), he deposits another $100, and at the end of that year, he withdraws $20 in interest. He continues the process year after year, adding $100 to his account each January 1 and withdrawing all the interest at the year-end. Each January 1, his cumulative deposit is $100 greater than the year before, and each December 31 the interest withdrawal is $10 greater than the year before. In the tenth year, he deposits $100 (for a total of $1,000), and at the end of the year, he withdraws $100. In that year, therefore, his interest equals his new deposit.

Every year thereafter, he continues to deposit $100, but he withdraws a larger amount: $110, then $120, and so on. Suddenly, he is accused of "decapitalizing" the bank. Of course, he is not doing so, for the appropriate comparison is not between his interest and his *new* deposit, but between his interest and the cumulative amount deposited over the years. The same is true for MNCs investing in LDCs. The amounts earned as profits should be compared with the cumulative investment over the years, which presumably is producing goods and services sufficient to yield the profit.

The Balance of Payments. The other process concerns the balance of payments. Even though profits may be justified by cumulative investment, the excess of profit payment over investment inflow may present a cash flow problem. Do MNCs cause a drain on a country's foreign exchange?

Here also there is more than meets the eye. MNCs produce export goods, which bring foreign exchange earnings to their host countries. They also produce import substitutes, which save foreign exchange. The proper comparison, therefore, is between the two columns below:

MNCs provide (or save) foreign exchange for host countries by	MNCs use the foreign exchange of host countries by
1. bringing in new investment.	1. remitting profits to the home companies.
2. exporting.	2. importing supplies, etc.
3. producing for the home market goods that otherwise would have been imported.	

Without special studies (which we believe have not been made), it is not possible to know the balance (positive or negative) of this comparison. Vernon (1971, p. 174) makes some estimates of the impact U.S. MNCs have on the balance of payments of LDCs. With the most reasonable of assumptions (that MNCs do export and do cause import substitution to some degree), the total balance-of-payments impact turns out positive, sometimes heavily so.

In summary, the proposition that "MNCs take out more than they put in" appears to be based on a confusion of two principles—one relating to the rate of return, and the other the balance of payments—each of which is based on flawed reasoning.

7. They Don't Really Provide Capital; They Acquire It Locally

Quoting from a number of studies, Barnet and Müller (1974, p. 153) show that from 1957 to 1965, "U.S.-based global corporations financed 83 percent of their Latin American investments locally, either from reinvested earnings or from local Latin American savings." Later on the same page, they say that "a primary purpose is to take such {reinvested} earnings out of the country as fast as possible."

Again, Barnet and Müller appear to be criticizing MNCs for two actions that are opposite to one another—for reinvesting their earnings and for taking them out of the country. It is, of course, impossible to do both with the same earnings.

But what about the other part of their argument—that MNCs generate substantial amounts of capital locally? In most LDCs, they are required to be 51 percent national. Since MNCs do not give away their stock, they must sell it, thus raising capital locally. They also borrow from local banks. Companies the world over borrow working capital from banks in the same city where they are located as it makes sense to get credit from institutions they are in frequent contact with.

But Barnet and Müller—and other critics—draw two improper con- clusions from this state of events. One is that "global corporations are not in fact major suppliers of finance capital to poor countries" (1974, p. 153), and in one sense, this statement is true. Long before MNCs began to be heavily criticized, it was recognized that most investment in LDCs is generated locally—some 90 percent or so, depending on the country. Reasonable analysts have never suggested that MNCs are or should be the principal purveyors of capital to LDCs, but the marginal 2 percent or so that they do supply may be important. Furthermore, if a company supplies $1,000 of foreign capital and then borrows $2,000 locally to make the operation work, it has still supplied the $1,000. This type of outside assistance is all MNCs have ever claimed, and to imply that they have done otherwise is misleading.

The second improper assumption is that MNCs repatriate the profits earned on capital borrowed in LDCs. Quite the contrary. If the locally provided capital is in the form of equity capital (shares of stock), MNCs pay dividends to the local investors; if it is borrowed capital, they pay interest to the local lender.

A further criticism is that MNCs frequently buy local companies rather than start new ones, so they are not really adding to the productive capacity of the host country. Forgotten is the fact that the MNCs must pay the sellers of those enterprises, who thereby have the wherewithal to invest anew. *Any* capital brought in from abroad, whether invested in a new enterprise or an old one, helps increase the productive capacity of the host country.

There is, however, one point on which we join the critics. In many LDCs, governments have held interest rates artificially low, ostensibly to encourage development by local companies as well as foreign ones. We believe this practice is one of the ways in which LDC governments have harmed their poor: By making capital cheap, they promote capital- intensive instead of labor-intensive investment. Since officials in LDCs often borrow from the same government entities whose policies they control (conflict-of-interest laws are scarce), it is to their personal advantage to keep the rates low. But it is hard to keep rates low for themselves without according the same facilities to MNCs. If an MNC can borrow at 6 percent in a given LDC, why would the company bring capital in from New York where borrowing might cost 15 or even 20 percent?

Although we agree with the critics of this practice, we differ in placing the responsibility. It lies squarely with the governments of LDCs, not with the MNCs.

8. *They Minimize Their Taxes Through Transfer Pricing*

One of the sharpest criticisms of MNCs is that their subsidiaries do business with their parent companies at transfer (or other-than-market) prices. If a subsidiary in a LDC wishes to transfer its recorded profit to the home country (because taxes on profits are less there), the subsidiary will be overcharged by its parent company for the subsidiary's imports and undercharge for its exports to the parent company. By the former act, the subsidiary increases its own costs (while increasing the revenue of the parent); by the latter act, it decreases its revenues (while decreasing the costs for its parent). By both actions, the subsidiary decreases its own profit, and increases the profit of the parent company. Therefore, the LDC government is deprived of a profits tax, which is transferred to the country of the parent company.

There are two ways to investigate transfer pricing. One is by directly comparing the prices charged by MNCs (parents and subsidiaries) with the market prices. We have heard of a number of such studies, but it would appear that any such effort would be fraught with danger. First, how do the researchers gain access to the records of the companies? Second, how can we be sure that the correct market prices are used for the comparison? Often products differ in quality, and comparative prices must be quoted for specific locations and specific times.

Vernon (1971, p. 139) quotes different studies that indicate clearly that transfer pricing does occur. Sometimes, he concludes, transfer pricing is utilized because an LDC government has placed a ceiling on profit transmission by usual means. Vernon suggests that host governments may not be able to control whether profits are repatriated, only the form in which repatriation occurs.

The second way to investigate transfer pricing would be to examine the tax laws of different countries to see whether there is a motive for persistent transfer in one direction. Vernon (1971) has also made such an examination, and he has concluded that tax laws differ so widely that sometimes there is a motive to shift profits form LDCs to MDCs and sometimes there is a motive to shift profits the other way around. Thus, he says, "the cases so far uncovered do not create the basis for assuming that there is a systematic bias in favor of assigning the largest profit to the parent" (p. 139).

Even if transfer pricing were practiced to the detriment of LDC governments, they are not without defenses. All goods must cross their frontiers, and most are valued by a customs agent. By hiring the appropriate experts (national or foreign), a government may make its own comparison of prices on the company books and those quoted internationally, and it may then tax the difference to the extent that is required to discourage the practice.

9. They Maximize Global Profits, Not Profits in the LDCs

A further criticism is that MNCs maximize their global profits instead of the profits of a subsidiary within a given LDC. For example, an MNC might forbid a subsidiary to export from its host country, so that the market might be safeguarded for the parent company.

There is, however, little hard evidence on the extent to which this practice occurs. It is also difficult to understand *why* it would occur. If MNCs are profit minded (as most of the critics aver), why would they not export from the most advantageous country, whether this happened to be the country of the parent or that of the subsidiary?

The question is whether decision making is decentralized. Barnet and Müller (1974) assert that it is not, and they cite a number of anecdotes. Osborn, Garnier, Arias, and Lecon (1978) questioned a large number of officials (virtually all Mexican) of U.S.-affiliated companies in Mexico and concluded that the range of decisions made by the Mexicans is much wider than is normally supposed.

The evidence is insufficient for any categorical judgment, and we can only conclude that the theoretical underpinnings for this complaint are shaky and empirical evidence is scant.

10. They Use Capital-Intensive Methods of Production

It is often suggested that MNCs use machinery (capital-intensive methods) when they might employ labor instead (labor-intensive methods) so that they aggravate the already serious unemployment in LDCs. The United Nations (1974, p. 69) reports that "in general, multinational corporations tend to reproduce technologies which they have already developed and which they are already using in their home countries. These are apt to be capital intensive."

But the United Nations report does not tell us how this opinion was reached, and a survey of studies gives mixed results. The International Labor Organization (in an unpublished background report for a study on employment conditions in Kenya: ILO 1972) found that the technology of MNCs in Kenya tends to be more labor intensive than that of the home companies and also more labor intensive than Kenyan companies producing the same goods. Morley and Smith (1977, p. 261) found that MNCs in Brazil utilize significantly more labor-intensive techniques than their home companies do. Von Bertrab-Erdman (1968) found similar results for European companies operating in Latin America, and Strassman (1968) found MNCs using secondhand, labor-intensive equipment in

Mexico but felt his sample was too small for generalization. On the other hand, Mason (n.d.), Yoeman (1968), Reuber (1973), and Wells (1973) all studied enterprises that did use their home-country methods with little adaptation. Vernon (1971, p. 182) believes that because of their concern for quality control and their aversion to risk, MNCs may tend toward home-country technologies in their central processes but that in peripheral operations, they may use more labor-intensive techniques.

The number of studies is too small to make generalizations, so we can only conclude that the jury is still out. Even if MNCs do employ capital-intensive techniques, it is not at all clear that they are more capital intensive than similar techniques of national companies. So we ask, Why do *any* companies choose the technologies that they do?

The most likely answer is that they respond to local conditions and especially to government policy. In their quest for development over the past thirty years, most LDC governments have followed a number of policies that tend to make all modern companies (whether national or MNC) lean toward capital-intensive technology. We have already mentioned the high wages, exclusive unions, and the low interest rates. In addition, LDC governments have awarded tax holidays and customs-duty preferences to companies importing machinery, and they have protected their countries' markets by establishing high tariffs and exchange controls on competing goods. The policies of LDC governments have therefore been strongly prejudiced toward capital-intensive production, whether by local concerns or by MNCs. In an earlier work (Loehr and Powelson 1981, pp. 171–178), we cite a number of studies to support this generalization.

In summary, we are not at all sure that MNCs do in fact use more capital-intensive techniques in LDCs than they do at home, or that they use more than the national companies do. The studies so far would indicate that some do and some do not. But certainly, LDC governments have supplied every incentive for both MNCs and national companies to employ capital-intensive methods. It does not appear fair to give lollipops for unsavory behavior and then to condemn the recipients for how they act.

11. Their Technology Is Inappropriate

Critics often try to discredit the earlier wisdom that MNCs are a major source of technology flow to LDCs. Their arguments are, first, it is the wrong kind of technology; second, it costs too much.

Before dealing with these criticisms, let us clarify our own view of technology transfer. For centuries, technology has been carried from countries of origin to other countries that have adopted and adapted it. In an earlier era, technology was spread by traders (as from China to the Middle East along the silk route); in medieval times and later, it traveled with craftsmen. More often than not, the technology had to be adapted to local conditions. For example, the early settlers in the United States had to alter machines so they burned wood instead of coal as in England.

We do not think the situation has basically changed. We favor the interaction of peoples and the spread of knowledge, although we must remember that, historically, technology is location-specific. This point is readily observed in agriculture, as different soils, climates, and other natural conditions have required that miracle seeds developed in one country be redeveloped in another. Instead of seeds themselves, the earlier research and development contributed the framework for localized research. The same point may be less obvious in industry, but it is no less true.

Today, MNCs are the principal vehicle for the transfer of industrial technology. But the conventional form of that transfer that is attacked by the critics—the sale of patent rights—is probably the least significant. More important is the communication of business methods such as management, accounting, and salesmanship, which are absorbed on a day-to-day basis by nationals who work for MNCs. These nationals may then form businesses of their own, adapting the techniques to their own needs. That this form of transfer goes on all the time is obvious, but it is not considered "exciting" enough for research. Hence, we know little about how much of it occurs.

On patents, we tend to agree with the critics in all respects except we wonder what the problem is. We especially agree that the technology supplied by MNCs is often the wrong kind—too capital intensive— and that therefore, it should not be bought by anyone in LDCs. We agree that LDCs would do well to develop their own research more than they have. But if these arguments are true, why fuss over the fact that the wrong technology costs too much? Could it not be argued that LDCs are *better* off this way since the situation encourages them to develop their own substitutes?

In the extractive industries, where the companies are increasingly being nationalized, a new basis for technology transfer is being worked out. Earlier, technology may have been supplied by parent to subsidiary or from a subsidiary in one country to a subsidiary in another. Now that there are few subsidiaries, contracts are increasingly being written between the new national companies and the old foreign ones. These contracts deal not only with technology, but also with consulting and capital. The new companies may even draw up contracts with the competitors of the old foreign producers. We laud these changes, which increase the bargaining advantage of the national companies.

The same type of action is not so well advanced in manufacturing. Manufacturers with subsidiaries in LDCs may be reluctant to sell patents to competitors of their subsidiaries, and, surely, if they do sell a patent outside the family, they are likely to stipulate that the buyer cannot export the manufactured product. Barnet and Müller (1974, p. 163) make a big point of this stipulation, but we accept it as a fact of life. International patent laws have been worked out over the centuries so that compromises have been made between rewarding the inventors and diffusing the products. We doubt that a new international order will suddenly change the terms, and we are not convinced that it is desirable to change them. We would rather encourage a new generation of inventors in LDCs, who would themselves be rewarded and protected by the international patent laws.

12. They Employ Nationals from Their Home Countries

Three decades ago, it was customary to fault MNCs for failing to promote host-country nationals to responsible positions. Employment was thus two tiered: executives from the home country and blue-collar workers from the host country.

That criticism is not much heard any more, for the situation has greatly changed. In Mexico, no foreigner may be hired unless it can be proved that there is no Mexican capable of doing the job. Since the government resists such "proofs" strongly, virtually all MNC-affiliated companies in Mexico are staffed by Mexicans, from the chairman of the board on down. Other LDCs have not gone so far, and sometimes high positions are still filled from home, but the tendency is definitely toward host-country hiring. According to a United Nations report on MNCs (1973, p. 53), "an OECD study shows that for a sample of 50 foreign investment projects, local clerks and accountants accounted for 97 percent of the staff concerned, foremen and supervisors 90 percent, sales and marketing personnel 80 percent, management and engineering personnel 73 percent. There is, moreover, a tendency for the local share to increase over time, especially in the professional categories." The same report indicates (p. 53) that "many managers and technicians move from foreign affiliates to domestic enterprises," thus applying their experience to the development of home industries.

Comparative salaries are still hotly debated, however. It is often charged that MNCs pay higher salaries to home-country personnel than to host-country personnel for the same work. Since we have found no data to substantiate this charge, we do not know to what extent it is true. If it is true, however, the increased hiring of host-country personnel should solve the matter. Our informal understanding (unresearched) is that it is increasingly difficult to find a situation in which home-country and host-country personnel are in fact doing the same work. Why would a profit-seeking MNC hire from its home country if the same task could be performed cheaper by a host-country employee?

The problem that does remain, however, is that there is a wide gap between host-country and home-country salaries. If a home-country employee is to be attracted, the company must pay a salary comparable to what its competitors would pay at home. But salaries paid to host-country employees must be lower, or else they will not conform to alternative opportunities and distortions will be created.

Possibly the problem will be resolved when only host-country nationals are employed, as in Mexico. But we have a nagging doubt here just as we believe that the scarcity of high-level personnel in LDCs leads to similar disparities between blue-collar and executive employment in local industries (although once again we have seen no data). Thus, the problem is probably not confined to MNCs, and most likely it will not be resolved until a greater supply of executive talent can be trained.

We deduce from this assessment that the disparities are structural. A new economic order will not affect them.

13. They Transmit the Culture of Their Home Countries

Our personal inclination might be to sympathize with the criticism that MNCs transmit the culture of their home countries to host countries. There are many aspects of our own country's culture that we do not make a part of our lives, but we do not patronizingly view our fellow creatures whose tastes are different, nor do we judge them incapable of resisting—if they so choose—the cultural demands that constantly bombard them. Although we have heard the Coca-Cola syndrome proclaimed by many writers (including Barnet and Müller 1974, p. 173), none that we know of has offered a workable "solution."

Culture—good and bad—has always been transmitted by interpersonal contact. Some of the degeneracy of court life in France during the ancien régime was spread to England, Prussia, and Spain without MNCs to carry it there. Because of technological breakthroughs in the media, news travels more rapidly than ever, and ideas are picked up everywhere. We even have some doubt that Coca-Cola is a multinational enterprise since we understand it is produced by local companies who buy the extract from the U.S. company and do their own advertising.[1] Are we to propose that either this practice, or the spreading of fashions through the media, should be restricted through an international code of conduct drawn up by some "culture czars"?

To some extent, governments in LDCs already possess tools to control activities or products that are incompatible with cultural norms. Consumption taxes can be imposed on goods and services considered offensive. Public regulation in developing countries is common. Local governments are best able to decide which goods and services are not desirable and limit them accordingly. Indeed, international controls on MNC activities would be oppressive if they denied certain goods and services to LDCs that want them.

14. They Bribe Government Officials

Bribery of LDC officials, by officers of MNCs, is frequent and well documented. It falls within a general aura of corruption, which is perhaps the most serious and least studied obstacle to economic development. Scholars ignore it (for how can it be examined scientifically?), and journalists revel in it. The *New York Times* has written about corruption in Algeria (Oct. 5, 1979), Costa Rica (Dec. 15, 1980), Honduras (Dec. 23, 1980), Indonesia (June 3, 1979), Iran (March 2, 1979; Jan. 11, 1981), the Ivory Coast (Nov. 9, 1980), Mexico (Dec. 16, 1979; Jan. 11, 1981), Nigeria (Oct. 24, 1979; Sept. 25, 1980), Uganda (Dec. 14, 1980), Venezuela (May 10, 1980), and Zaire (March 6, 1979; Nov. 13, 1979), to name only a few of the articles.

The first reason given for an international code of conduct of MNCs is to "prevent interference in the internal affairs of the countries where they operate." How do the MNCs interfere? Presumably, by bribing government officials to grant them licenses or tax privileges, to permit repatriation of profits, to relax price and wage regulations, or to pass special legislation in their favor.

How is bribery controlled in industrialized countries? Perhaps the controversial Abscam investigation in the United States (1980-1981) is instructive. Posing as rich Arabs wanting privileges or contracts, law enforcement officials tempted congressmen and then prosecuted those who succumbed. Instead of seeking the offerers of bribes, they pursued the *recipients*. Under NIEO, the approach would be the other way around.

Not only would the recipients of bribes remain untouched, but their power to demand bribes would be enhanced. The same granters or deniers of privilege would be the ones to enforce the code of conduct— here indeed is the fox tending the chicken coop! By placing more power into the hands of government officials, NIEO would create a greater potential for corruption, not less.

Corruption in LDCs will end when the people of the LDCs, through their appropriate authorities, demand that it end—no earlier, no later. Without infringing on the sovereignty of LDCs, there is absolutely nothing that outsiders can do. The U.S. government may legislate against bribery by U.S. enterprises in LDCs, and we favor the idea behind such legislation; but it would infringe on the countries concerned, for the U.S. government would be declaring itself a court of justice for events occurring on the territory of others.

In summary, corruption is a problem of underdevelopment; it may even be *the* problem. It pervades LDCs, being practiced by government officials, citizens, foreigners, local companies, and MNCs. The solution to the problem already lies within the power of LDC governments, when and if they are ready to use it. Until that moment, however, no international code of conduct will help. If such a code were enforceable by LDC government officials, we suspect it might even inflame the situation it would be trying to correct.

15. They Collaborate with Racist Regimes and Colonial Administrations

Another reason put forward for a code of conduct is to prevent MNC "collaboration with racist regimes." "Racist regimes" clearly refers to one country, South Africa. The term does not refer to Kenya, Tanzania, or Uganda for discriminating against their peoples of Indian origin; nor Ethiopia for discriminating against non-Amharics; nor West African countries for discriminating against their peoples of Lebanese origin; nor Liberia for discriminating (before the coup of 1980) against citizens blacker than the government officials or (after the coup) against those not so black as the government officials; nor India for discriminating against the lower castes and Muslims in the state of Bihar. The term does not refer to the many African governments that assign privileges on the basis of tribe, nor to Latin American countries in which access to economic advantage may depend on how Spanish or Portuguese one is, as opposed to how Indian or how black.

If NIEO were ever tested in an international court, we foresee interminable arguments over the definition of "racism," and over how "racist" a regime must be in order to be convicted.

Also because governments that support NIEO are not willing to be judged in an international court themselves, of course they must also leave jurisdiction on racism in South Africa to the South African government. And therein lies the rub.

Curiously, the MNCs in South Africa behave "better" with respect to racism than the national companies do. This statement is not under dispute; the controversy centers on "how much better." In 1977, a black minister from Philadelphia, Leon Sullivan, drew up a code of conduct for the 350-odd U.S. companies operating in South Africa; within a year, over 100 had agreed to abide by it. The code calls for "total desegregation of eating, work and toilet facilities in plants; equal employment opportunities; comparable pay for all employees in the same jobs; development of apprentice and management trainee programs for nonwhites; promotion of blacks and colored to higher posts; improvement of employees' living conditions; and support for unionization efforts by nonwhites" (*Time* Sept. 18, 1978, p. 66). In the same article, *Time* reported that

> Ford deserves top marks for doing away with the most noxious symbols of apartheid.... Colgate Palmolive ... assumed most of the costs of operating a black township school in a neighboring community to ensure higher educational standards for nonwhites.... While a very few firms, notably IBM, have long had equal-pay-equal-work policies, many more companies have lately been moving to redress a particular grievance of blacks: a system of bonuses that traditionally allowed whites to earn [more than blacks in similar jobs}.... Mobil ... has also striven to train and promote nonwhites. Now most of the supervisory jobs at the Mobil refineries in Cape Town and Durban are held by nonwhites.

Still, many people are not satisfied with the efforts that have been made, including the Reverend Sullivan himself, who chastized General Motors at a stockholders' meeting in 1980 for its failure to make greater progress (*New Yorker* Dec. 22, 1980, p. 25).

Among the opponents of apartheid is South Africa's largest business enterprise, the Anglo-American Corporation, a giant mining company (gold and diamonds) formerly owned by the late Harry Oppenheimer, who "spent millions of dollars of his own and the company's money to improve black education, housing, and other interests" (*New York Times* Aug. 16, 1977). However, those efforts so angered the government that in 1977, it blocked a major deal for Anglo-American to take over another large company, the South African Manganese Amcor, Ltd.

All the changes are cosmetic only, NIEO advocates aver, for to date, they have affected only a small number of black employees. We agree about the horrors of apartheid, and we agree that progress is slow. But flowers do not come full-blown, and the people who would stamp out the first sprouts because they are not big enough will never see the blossoms. Likewise, once a naughty child does something right, we praise it for its tiny progress rather than only blame it for its continued wrongs. Because MNCs are behaving better than what will replace them if they are withdrawn (national companies), we are reluctant to respond to their moves with punishing controls, especially when the South African government would be the enforcer.

16. They Steal Land

Plantation-type MNCs are frequently charged with stealing land from ignorant peasants in the LDCs. This practice especially occurs when illiterate peasants are using land under customary entitlement: Their families have lived on it and farmed it for centuries. Suddenly, the government passes title laws, and all lands must be registered. The peasants, unfamiliar with the laws, do nothing, and then they may discover that the land has been registered under someone else's name, possibly a multinational producer of, say, fruit. Soldiers come, and the peasants are evicted.

Henry Kamm wrote as follows in the *New York Times* (Jan. 29, 1981):

> The struggle began about 10 years ago, when sugar prices were high and the upland regions of Negros Island had not yet been planted with cane. That land suddenly had a much higher value for those who wanted to expand their holdings or start sugar plantations.
>
> The highlands had been populated for years by subsistence farmers, often from other islands. Poor and ignorant of the formalities involved, they never acquired title to their land.
>
> The practice known throughout the Philippines as land-grabbing took hold. People in the area who were versed in the legal formalities and ready with a bribe obtained titles to land long tilled by others.
>
> "Suddenly you find the land that your family has been farming for 40 years has been titled to someone else's name," the Rev. Edgar Saguisin said. "The scars of the dispute are so deep."

Merida Welles reports (*New York Times* Feb. 15, 1981) that lands claimed for generations by Indians in Brazil were conceded, early in the sixties, to a Brazilian company in which a major international tobacco company holds a considerable interest.

We find this land-grabbing practice unconscionable. We fear, however, that if the stealing is tagged exclusively to MNCs, and if it is supposed that a government-enforced code of conduct will end it, then vigilance will be relaxed at the very point it needs to be strengthened.

Stealing land through sophisticated legalism is an age-old practice. It was done by Romans and Greeks; by Chinese during many dynasties; by Spaniards, Portuguese, and Dutch in Latin America and Africa; and by the Americans who seized Liberia in the nineteenth century. At approximately the same time as the last, it was being done by *caudillos* associated with Porfirio Diaz in Mexico. It can be done today in Brazil and the Philippines (or any other LDC) only with the support (or at least acquiescence) of the government. An international code of conduct enforced by a LDC government once again brings the fox to the chicken coop.

How Do the Criticisms Balance Out?

The MNC emerges still strong from the discussion of the sixteen criticisms, but a bit deflated. MNCs are not so mobile as is often assumed; they pay too high wages instead of "exploiting" their employees; mineral MNCs are mostly nationalized or in the process of being nationalized; manufacturing MNCs do not earn excessive profits and tend to reinvest them in the host country; their choice of labor- or capital-intensive methods and their use of domestic capital are not capricious but respond to the policy incentives of LDC governments; MNCs increasingly employ host-country nationals in high positions; they do not automatically send to home countries the earnings on capital borrowed in host countries. They sometimes maximize global profits at the expense of the host countries, but not always—and without further research, we do not know which situation dominates. MNCs do use transfer pricing, but the benefits are likely to be transferred to the host country as well as to the home country.

Some complaints, such as bribery and land stealing, are fully justified. In all such cases, however, these injustices are widely practiced, not just by MNCs. Being partisans of equal justice for all, we are dubious about a code of conduct that would condemn certain institutions and not others for committing specific transgressions. The practice itself, not just a particular perpetrator of it, should be condemned. The charges against MNCs that most require scrutiny—and to us, are the most offensive— are the very ones that would continue to be practiced widely by others even if they were outlawed for MNCs.

We see the current campaign against MNCs as an inadvertent, unholy alliance between partisans of equity and justice (especially NIEO advocates in MDCs) on the one hand, and powerful interest groups and government officials in LDCs on the other, who would like to subdue the MNCs so that they themselves can take over the unsavory practices that a code of conduct would outlaw for MNCs.

How Is "the Belief" Sustained?

"The belief" about the extraordinary powers of multinational corporations is reinforced by a number of statistical devices to which unwary audiences—especially those composed of uncritical believers—may readily fall prey. These devices include selective perception and wrong comparisons, both of which contribute to a general momentum that lulls the reader's capacity to perceive inconsistencies. These devices are not peculiar to the issue of MNCs; they are present in many popular articles that attempt to make economic points on emotionally charged issues.

An author who wishes to show that MNCs specialize in capital-intensive methods cites only those studies that have reached this conclusion and ignores contrary ones (selective perception). If he wishes to "prove" that MNCs earn extraordinarily high profits, he cites only mineral (perhaps only petroleum) companies. At the least, he may combine mineral and manufacturing data, writing about the total as if they were homogeneous. Especially if he uses data since 1973 (when petroleum profits have been exorbitant), he can leave the impression that the profits of *all* MNCs are exorbitant.

A wrong comparison is made when profit remittances are compared with inflows of capital instead of with cumulative investment, or when the proceeds of exports (and other items) are omitted from the balance of payments. One example of a wrong comparison occurs in Barnet and Müller (1974, p. 322), who try to refute the argument that by buying from Japan, MNCs provide the U.S. consumer with cheaper products. That argument is "weak," the authors say, and cite data on three products imported by Westinghouse. They show that a certain portable radio commanded a price of $21.35 at the U.S. port, whereas the suggested retail price was $59.95. (The other two products had similar markups.) The markup of 188 percent is intended to show that U.S. consumers actually pay high prices for Japanese goods imported by MNCs.

There are two reasons why that example is a wrong comparison. First, the suggested retail price is rarely (if ever) paid; it is a reference price from which substantial discounts are made. Second, the markup includes all the expenses of sales and delivery, and we are not told how much these are or how they would compare with the same expenses for a U.S.-made product. Finally, we do not know whether the markups on the three Westinghouse products are average for all such products, or whether the authors selectively perceived the greatest. To the unskilled reader, the data may appear convincing; in fact, however, they tell us nothing at all.

We are more impressed by the fact that U.S. consumers do buy imports from Japan, and we presume the reason is that they are of high quality and cheaper than any alternative.

Another frequent wrong comparison is one that is used to prove that producers of primary products receive only a small proportion of the total sale price. For example, this comparison was made by Laszlo et al. (1980, p. 41):

> The producing country receives a low percentage of earnings out of the sales price charged in the consuming country. Thus, in the period from 1967–1972, the export price as a percentage of the final sales price was 53 percent in the case of tea, 15 percent for cocoa (both as a percentage

of the United Kingdom price), 48 percent for peanut oil, 30 percent for
citric juices, 20 percent for bananas, 14 percent for coffee, 32 percent for
jute, 55 percent for copper concentrate, 75 percent for refined tin (in
these seven cases, as a percentage of the price in France), and 10 percent
for iron ore (Federal Republic of Germany prices). Since the export price
includes all the local costs, the primary producers earn only a small
percentage of the final sales price, while the transnational corporations—
through their peculiar purchasing mechanisms—obtain the biggest share.

Thus, the amount received by the producing company is compared to
the sales price charged in the consuming country without regard to the
selling company's costs outside the producing country.

Now, it may be reasonable to criticize an MNC for paying too low
a price to the producing country, but if one does so, one must also
show that the low price is not justified by the division of costs. If the
costs of transport, storage, processing, canning, delivery to the grocery
store, and retailing happen to be 80 percent of the final price, and if
the consumer will pay no more than that final price (because if the
price were higher, he would choose something else), then the primary
producer must take 20 percent or his product will never reach the
market at all. Merely to say that transnational corporations receive the
biggest share "through their peculiar purchasing mechanisms" is too
vague an explanation for a serious economic disquisition. It also fails
to take into account that much of that share is paid out for transport
and other services, and thus, the MNC does not receive it at all.

When an author (or an audience) is in the mood to hear anything
bad about MNCs, so that selective perception and wrong comparisons
are acceptable, then inconsistencies are ignored. We have seen that
Barnet and Müller have criticized MNCs for paying wages that are too
high and wages that are too low; they criticized them for both reinvesting
their profits in the host countries and for distributing them to the home
countries. Much of the momentum in the campaign to discredit MNCs
has been achieved by addressing audiences who were already negatively
disposed toward MNCs and not sufficiently critical to check for inconsistencies in the material presented.

In such an atmosphere, multinational enterprises become responsible
for everything the author does not like.

The Coca-Cola syndrome is another case in point. To some people,
soft drinks are a symbol of Western degeneracy. To blame the spread
of "degenerate" human behavior on one out of several channels through
which it is transmitted, rather than to search for its psychological causes,
appears to us an unproductive way to approach or even to define a
problem. The paradox is heightened because—as we have pointed out—
it is doubtful that Coca-Cola is a large multinational enterprise at all.

Conclusion

This chapter has not been written out of any love of multinational enterprises. We despise some of their practices, such as bribery and "legal" land stealing. Real problems exist—problems of poverty, maldistribution, and injustice—and MNCs are associated with them. But if MNCs are always presented as the sole source of those problems, and if information is selectively perceived to support that distortion, then we will have a running start on finding solutions to them—but in the wrong direction.

MNCs are already restricted by a number of forces, some of them economic, some institutional. Among the latter, stronger LDC governments figure prominently. MNCs also respond to economic policies, just as other companies and individuals do. We do not find them so powerful as to warrant special controls, national or international.

We have, however, a more philosophical motive for opposing the NIEO code of conduct. We believe in equality before the law: A practice to be outlawed should be outlawed for all. We favor an international code to eliminate bribery and to protect the ignorant from the predations of the sophisticated, but applying such a code differentially to some institutions would merely encourage other institutions to continue or begin the undesired practices.

We suspect that if a universally applicable code were introduced into NIEO and that if governments of LDCs suspected that their own activities might therefore be limited, they would lose some of their enthusiasm.

Notes

1. According to the Coca-Cola Company's annual report of December 31, 1978, 90 percent of the syrup and concentrate is sold for further processing outside the company before sale to the ultimate consumer. In Latin America, the final product is marketed through 240 bottling companies, most of which are owned and operated by citizens of the countries concerned. In the Europe and Africa division, most of 460 bottling plants are owned and operated by citizens of the countries concerned, although 12 bottling and 4 canning plants are owned by the company. In the Pacific group, 23 out of the 210 bottling and canning plants are owned and operated by the company, the rest by citizens. We do not consider this information a major point in our argument, however. The essential point is that people who see Coca-Cola as the spread of a degenerate culture would do better to persuade the world of a more nutritive substitute rather than complain about one vehicle (a multinational corporation?) through which culture is spread. No country is coerced to buy, drink, or display the signs of Cola-Cola.

APPENDIX

TABLE 4A.1
U.S. Direct Investment Position at Year-End in Less Developed Countries, 1966-1979 (Millions of $)

Year	All Industries	Petroleum	Manufacturing	Other
1966	13,866	5,051	3,525	5,290
1967	14,905	5,289	3,891	5,725
1968	16,497	5,852	4,439	6,206
1969	17,627	6,032	5,047	6,548
1970	19,193	6,644	5,477	7,072
1971	20,719	7,027	6,038	7,654
1972	22,273	7,376	6,767	8,130
1973	22,904	6,074	7,820	9,010
1974	19,848	-390	9,200	11,038
1975	26,288	2,519	10,459	13,310
1976	29,312	2,690	11,395	15,227
1977	34,462	3,520	12,324	18,618
1978	40,400	4,361	14,223	21,816
1979	47,841	7,231	16,198	24,412

Source: Obie G. Whichard, "U.S. Direct Investment in 1979." Survey of Current Business 60:8 (August 1980) 16-37. Washington, D.C.: U.S. Department of Commerce.

TABLE 4A.2
Earnings on U.S. Direct Investments in LDCs, 1966-1979 (Millions of $)

Year		All Industries	Petroleum	Manufacturing	Other
1966	Reinvested	427	68	199	160
	Repatriated	1,946	1,229	132	584
	Total earnings	2,373	1,297	331	744
1967	Reinvested	297	33	116	148
	Repatriated	2,171	1,382	168	621
	Total earnings	2,468	1,415	284	769
1968	Reinvested	480	51	240	188
	Repatriated	2,430	1,580	203	646
	Total earnings	2,910	1,631	443	834
1969	Reinvested	420	-62	321	161
	Repatriated	2,652	1,684	206	762
	Total earnings	3,072	1,622	527	923
1970	Reinvested	601	71	322	208
	Repatriated	2,340	1,496	248	596
	Total earnings	2,941	1,567	570	804
1971	Reinvested	557	102	297	158
	Repatriated	2,712	1,895	258	559
	Total earnings	3,269	1,997	555	717
1972	Reinvested	795	42	435	319
	Repatriated	3,079	2,213	289	576
	Total earnings	3,874	2,255	724	895

Table 4A.2 cont.

1973	Reinvested	1,568	494	619	454
	Repatriated	4,272	3,138	353	781
	Total earnings	5,840	3,632	972	1,235
1974	Reinvested	1,841	423	762	655
	Repatriated	6,086	4,230	421	1,436
	Total earnings	7,927	4,653	1,183	2,091
1975	Reinvested	3,083	1,241	910	932
	Repatriated	3,599	1,829	453	1,317
	Total earnings	6,682	3,070	1,363	2,249
1976	Reinvested	1,223	-370	648	945
	Repatriated	5,824	3,340	608	1,877
	Total earnings	7,047	2,970	1,256	2,822
1977	Reinvested	2,269	485	834	950
	Repatriated	5,673	3,011	539	2,122
	Total earnings	7,942	3,496	1,373	3,072
1978	Reinvested	2,864	396	1,319	1,149
	Repatriated	6,100	2,821	700	2,579
	Total earnings	8,964	3,217	2,019	3,728
1979	Reinvested	3,573	843	1,281	1,450
	Repatriated	9,162	5,335	1,006	2,821
	Total earnings	12,735	6,178	2,287	4,271

Source: Same as Table 4A.1

TABLE 4A.3
Rate of Return on U.S. Direct Investments in LDCs

Year	All Industries	Petroleum	Manufacturing	Other
1967	.17	.27	.08	.14
1968	.19	.29	.11	.14
1969	.18	.27	.11	.14
1970	.16	.25	.11	.12
1971	.16	.29	.10	.10
1972	.18	.31	.11	.11
1973	.26	.54	.13	.14
1974	.37	1.63	.14	.21
1975	.29	2.88	.14	.18
1976	.25	1.14	.11	.20
1977	.25	1.13	.12	.18
1978	.24	.82	.15	.18
1979	.29	1.07	.15	.18

Source: Same as Table 4A.1

TABLE 4A.4
U.S. Direct Investment Flows to LDCs Compared to Repatriated Earnings, 1966-1979 (Millions of $)

Year		All Industries	Petroleum	Manufacturing	Other
1966	Investment flows	499	-4	237	265
	Repatriated earnings	1,946	1,229	132	584
	Balance (flows less earnings)	-1,447	-1,233	105	-319
1967	Investment flows	734	222	264	247
	Repatriated earnings	2,171	1,382	168	621
	Balance (flows less earnings)	-1,437	-1,160	96	-374
1968	Investment flows	1,126	506	308	313
	Repatriated earnings	2,430	1,580	203	646
	Balance (flows less earnings)	-1,304	-1,074	105	-333
1969	Investment flows	738	249	286	202
	Repatriated earnings	2,652	1,684	206	762
	Balance (flows less earnings)	-1,914	-1,435	80	-560
1970	Investment flows	1,116	590	157	368
	Repatriated earnings	2,340	1,496	248	596
	Balance (flows less earnings)	-1,224	-906	-91	-228
1971	Investment flows	1,005	293	284	428
	Repatriated earnings	2,712	1,895	258	559
	Balance (flows less earnings)	-1,707	-1,602	26	-131
1972	Investment flows	816	329	323	164
	Repatriated earnings	3,078	2,213	289	576
	Balance (flows less earnings)	-2,263	-1,884	34	-412

1973	Investment flows	-852	-1,749	443	454
	Repatriated earnings	4,272	3,138	353	781
	Balance (flows less earnings)	-5,124	-4,887	90	-327
1974	Investment flows	-4,573	-6,881	670	1,638
	Repatriated earnings	6,086	4,230	421	1,436
	Balance (flows less earnings)	-10,659	-11,111	249	202
1975	Investment flows	3,732	1,988	379	1,365
	Repatriated earnings	3,599	1,829	453	1,317
	Balance (flows less earnings)	133	159	-74	48
1976	Investment flows	1,827	603	265	959
	Repatriated earnings	5,824	3,340	608	1,877
	Balance (flows less earnings)	-3,997	-2,737	-343	-918
1977	Investment flows	2,766	428	64	2,274
	Repatriated earnings	5,673	3,011	539	2,122
	Balance (flows less earnings)	-2,907	-2,583	-475	152
1978	Investment flows	2,864	554	503	1,808
	Repatriated earnings	6,100	2,821	700	2,579
	Balance (flows less earnings)	-3,236	-2,267	-197	-771
1979	Investment flows	3,749	2,088	688	972
	Repatriated earnings	9,162	5,335	1,006	2,821
	Balance (flows less earnings)	-5,413	-3,247	-318	-1,849

Source: Same as Table 4A.1

Note: Discrepancies in totals due to rounding.

Bibliography

Barnet, Richard J., and Müller, Ronald E. *Global Reach: The Power of the Multinational Corporations.* New York: Simon and Schuster, 1974.

International Labor Organization (ILO). *Employment, Incomes, and Equality: A Strategy for Increasing Productive Employment in Kenya.* Geneva, 1972.

————. *Wages and Working Conditions in Multinational Enterprises.* Geneva, 1976.

Laszlo, Ervin, et al. *The Obstacles to the New International Economic Order.* New York: Pergamon Press for United Nations Institute for Training and Research, 1980.

Loehr, William, and Powelson, John P. *The Economics of Development and Distribution.* New York: Harcourt, Brace, Jovanovich, 1981.

Mason, R. H. *The Transfer of Technology and the Factor Proportions Problem.* New York: United Nations, n.d.

Morley, Samuel A., and Smith, Gordon W. "The Choice of Technology: Multinational Firms in Brazil." *Economic Development and Cultural Change* 25:2 (January 1977), 239-264.

Osborn, Noel; Garnier, G.; Arias, F.; and Lecon, R. "Who Makes the Decisions?" *Mexican-American Review* (January 1978).

Reuber, Grant L. *Private Foreign Investment in Development.* London: Oxford University Press, 1973.

Strassman, W. Paul. *Technological Change and Economic Development: The Manufacturing Experience of Mexico and Puerto Rico.* Ithaca, N.Y.: Cornell University Press, 1968.

United Nations. *Multinational Corporations in World Development.* New York, 1973.

————. *The Acquisition of Technology from Multinational Corporations by Developing Countries.* New York, 1974.

United States, Department of Commerce (USDC). *Revised Data Series on U.S. Investment Abroad.* Washington, D.C., 1979.

Vernon, Raymond. *Sovereignty at Bay: The Multinational Spread of U.S. Enterprises.* New York: Basic Books, 1971.

Von Bertrab-Erdman, H. R. "The Transfer of Technology." Ph.D. dissertation, University of Texas, 1968.

Wells, Louis T. "Economic Man and Engineering Man." *Public Policy* 21:3 (Summer 1973), 319-342.

Whichard, Obie G. "U.S. Direct Investment in 1979." *Survey of Current Business* 60:8 (August 1980), 16-37. Washington, D.C.: Department of Commerce.

Yoeman, Wayne A. *Selection of Production Processes for the Manufacturing Subsidiaries of U.S. Based Multinational Corporations.* D.B.A. thesis, Harvard Business School, 1968.

5
International
Monetary Reform

The New International Economic Order calls for the "early estab-lishment of a link between Special Drawing Rights and additional development financing in the interest of developing countries, consistent with the monetary characteristics of Special Drawing Rights" (II, 1, f). Such an arrangement, together with a "full and effective participation of developing countries in all phases of decision-making for the formation of an equitable and durable monetary system" (II, 1, d), would probably cause a fundamental change in the character of the International Monetary Fund (IMF). Because the IMF is a keystone of the international monetary system, which MDC diplomats look on as vital to their own financial survival, such reforms must be minutely examined for unexpected side effects.

Established in 1944 at an international conference held in Bretton Woods, New Hampshire, the IMF was designed to avoid some of the problems of the 1930s. In the prewar period, international trade had plummeted during the Great Depression, trade protection had reached all-time highs, and chaos had reigned in foreign exchange markets. The framers of the Bretton Woods charter sought international economic stability and "rules of the game" that would help achieve efficient reconstruction and prosperity.

The Bretton Woods system performed that function well for over twenty-five years, after which time it was sharply altered by a worldwide liquidity crisis. Coincidentally with that crisis, LDCs were seeking to tie the IMF to concessionary financial aid. To understand the merits of the proposal for aid through the IMF, we must first understand the problems faced by the world monetary system. Therefore, we discuss this aspect before considering the LDC proposals for a link between the monetary system and foreign aid.

The Bretton Woods System

The Bretton Woods system was primarily concerned with monetary stability and efficient balance-of-payments adjustment. Through the IMF, the values of all major currencies were defined and fixed in terms of dollars. Dollars, in turn, were pegged to gold. Countries were expected to intervene in foreign exchange markets, buying or selling their own currency to prevent the fixed exchange rate from fluctuating beyond a fairly narrow range. An accepted international means of payment was required to provide stability for that system.

At the end of World War II, few nations possessed sufficient productive capacity to generate the confidence needed in their currencies if these were to be used as reserves. Only the U.S. dollar and the British pound originally commanded such confidence. The value of each was defined in gold, and each country maintained a gold stock sufficient to redeem its currency. During the 1950s, Britain was forced to do just that, i.e., exchange gold for pounds, and by the late 1950s, Britain had lost so much gold that there was only one reserve currency left, the U.S. dollar.

If the IMF system were to function properly, the United States had to have a balance-of-payments deficit, for only in that way would dollar reserves be created for other countries. Each IMF member (all MDCs and most LDCs, except Switzerland, China, and the Soviet bloc) was obliged to maintain reserves adequate to support the value of its currency.[1] In the case of a temporary balance-of-payments deficit, a country might borrow on a short-term basis from the IMF. Long-term (or fundamental) deficits were expected to be resolved by currency depreciation, with the permission of the IMF.

Thus, dollars were the primary means by which the Bretton Woods system functioned. As world trade prospered, the volume of transactions grew, and greater quantities of dollars were required to provide needed reserves. Since the U.S. balance-of-payments deficit was the only source of dollars, it grew to meet the demand for reserves. Indeed, even as late as the mid-1960s, economists were writing about a world "dollar shortage."

Special Drawing Rights

As the dollar liabilities of the United States came to exceed the U.S. gold supply (just as sterling liabilities had exceeded Britain's gold supply earlier), other countries began to lose confidence in the dollar as the only reserve currency. The U.S. inflation of the late sixties further eroded that confidence. Some economists also believed it was not "fair" for the United States to finance its deficit "free" by importing goods and services in exchange for dollar liabilities created by the stroke of a pen. For all these reasons, the agreement establishing the IMF was amended in 1967 to create a new reserve instrument called Special Drawing Rights (SDRs), and the amendment went into effect in 1969. SDRs are a reserve asset created by the IMF and distributed to members according to a formula based on their IMF quotas. Countries may use SDRs to settle payments imbalances.

SDRs are held only by the monetary authorities (usually the central banks) of member countries of the IMF. If a member country, A, requires some currency for settlement purposes, and if it has a balance of SDRs, then it can exchange the SDRs for the needed currency through the IMF. This situation would occur only if A had a deficit; countries with a surplus are required to give up excess currencies in exchange for SDRs. It is not necessary that the country receiving SDRs be the country issuing the currency required by A. The IMF surveys currency holdings by surplus countries and determines which country shall be required to accept SDRs from A. Users of SDRs (like A) are required to eventually replenish their holdings by returning a currency that is in short supply to the IMF. The IMF distributes the returned currency to countries that need it in exchange for SDRs. Countries like A pay an interest charge (currently 5 percent per year) on the SDRs they have used.

The creation of SDRs was an attempt to maintain the goals of the IMF and simultaneously to take some pressure off the dollar. SDRs supplement reserve assets so as to promote the orderly adjustment of exchange rates and balance of payments while maintaining a climate that is favorable to a healthy expansion of world trade (texts such as Scammell 1975 provide the details). At the same time, SDRs were expected to take the responsibility for reserve expansion away from the United States.

Problems with the Bretton Woods System

The original designers of the Bretton Woods system did not expect the great expansion of trade and payments that resulted from postwar reconstruction or the pressures that were placed on the United States. By 1958, European reconstruction was largely complete, and in that year, the EEC came into existence, and the last of the previously controlled European currencies became convertible. Japan was also entering world trade in a way that would have been unimaginable in 1944. Two "rounds" of tariff negotiations took place in the 1960s,[2] and they reduced trade barriers to new low levels, spurring an already rapidly growing world trade.

As that trade grew, so did the need for reserves. They were needed not only for trade, but also for supporting the pegged exchange rates. Set originally in 1944, the pegged values were revised infrequently. But with vast changes in the structure of international trade, the original values diverged further and further from what the market would have determined. Thus, increasing amounts of reserves were required simply to allow countries to honor their international commitments within the IMF.

In this context, SDRs were first issued in 1970-1972, at a bit over $3 billion per year.[3] Although SDRs were designed to replace the dollar as the reserve currency, they came a bit late. In August 1971, the convertibility of the dollar to gold was ended. The dollar was subsequently devalued, and by early 1973, currency values were determined by market forces. The pegged exchange rate system designed at Bretton Woods had ceased to exist; there was no longer a "key currency."

SDRs and the Link Proposal

As the Bretton Woods system was breaking down, LDCs proposed a link of SDRs to development aid. Similar proposals had accompanied earlier suggestions for monetary reform (Williamson 1977, pp. 81-85), but this time, the link proposal gathered force and received almost unanimous support from the LDCs. In mid-1972, the so-called Committee of Twenty[4] was established to suggest reforms, and the nine LDC representatives succeeded in obtaining a recommendation for the link.

The substance of the link proposal is as follows. The current allocation of SDRs, on the basis of IMF quotas, is designed to be "neutral" in that the quotas presumably reflect each country's need for reserves for adjustment purposes. Thus, most SDRs go to MDCs, since their quotas are the largest. The logic of this neutral distribution (as seen by MDC representatives) is expressed by analogy to some national monetary system. Suppose a country, X, whose currency is the peso, should double its money supply, and as a result, all prices doubled. Relative purchasing powers would remain unchanged only if each person were given one new peso for every peso already held; thus, the rich would receive more new pesos than the poor. If the new pesos were instead given disproportionately to some group (such as the poor), that group would be receiving a transfer of real purchasing power from all other groups. By the same token, new SDRs that are distributed to countries in rough proportion to their present reserve holdings do not redistribute real values of international reserves. The governments of LDCs, however, would like to arrange just such a redistribution. Hence, as part of NIEO, they have proposed there be a link between issues of SDRs and development aid.

The MDC representatives are wary of a system in which the number of SDRs issued might depend on the need for development assistance and not on the need for international reserves. But they might even be willing to accept such an arrangement—for after all, they currently contribute development assistance—except for other points LDCs have insisted on in the negotiations. Cline (1976, p. 51) makes the points:

- The "extra" SDRs (in excess of what they would receive under the current distribution plan) should be paid directly to LDCs and not through intermediaries such as the International Development Association—the "soft loan window" of the World Bank.
- The basis for distributing SDRs among LDCs would be their IMF quotas, with a somewhat larger allocation accruing to a limited list of LDLDCs.

The questions of whether there should be intermediaries or not and how the distributions of SDRs within LDCs should be made have caused debate, so we discuss them in turn.

Intermediary Institutions or Direct Link?

LDCs fear "control" by MDCs. Within the IMF, voting is weighted by quotas, so MDCs have most of the voting power. If the link occurred through some intermediary, such as the International Development Association (IDA), LDCs fear that MDCs would use their voting power to influence how the SDRs would be spent.

MDC representatives, on the other hand, emphasize that SDRs are not "free"; they represent the potential for a resource transfer (Cline 1976, p. 64). The MDCs, who would be providing the resources claimed through the spending of SDRs, seek some assurance that these resources would be put to good use, just as they uphold certain standards in other forms of aid. For example, nothing in the proposal would ensure that linked SDRs would be spent on investment rather than on consumption (Williamson 1977, pp. 92–93). The LDCs' insistence on receiving SDRs directly, when seen against the background of several LDCs whose governments have mismanaged their resources, reinforces MDC views that the SDRs might not be used for development.

But MDC concerns go even deeper. Currently, the MDCs are suffering from sluggish economic growth, inflation, and unemployment. They are seeking institutions—both international and domestic—to heal those problems, and they look to the IMF for possible relief. MDC representatives are sensitive to proposals that they feel might aggravate their problems or preclude their using an institution such as the IMF as a remedial tool. They express a general feeling that payments imbalances could be worsened by the link (as proposed), since LDCs would then have a way to avoid payments adjustments. Williamson (1977, p. 87) questions "whether it is proper to reward countries for failing to correct their [balance-of-payments] deficits" by distributing SDRs as aid without regard to performance.

Direct distribution of SDRs to LDCs without intermediate controls by multilateral agencies might weaken IMF control over destabilizing behavior and thereby prevent an efficient use of world resources. Currently, the IMF's ability to help a country with balance-of-payments problems is less constrained by funds than it is by the willingness of the country to agree on a policy package that would solve the problem if only it could be financed (Erb 1979, p. 400). Because of their confidence in the IMF's judgment, private lenders often come forth once such a policy package has been agreed upon, but only its strict standards maintain the IMF's credibility among private lenders. If the link were pursued without any IMF (or other multilateral) control over domestic policies, private sources of adjustment finance might be reduced, and SDRs might become a substitute for such private finance rather than a complement.

SDR Distribution Among LDCs

The proposed distribution of linked SDRs would benefit the more highly developed LDCs (Cline 1976, p. 94). IMF quotas closely reflect per capita income. Since the link proposal would allocate SDRs in rough proportion to the LDC quotas, by far the largest share would accrue to those LDCs that are already identified as NICs.[5] Indeed, if allocated by the plan proposed by the Committee of Twenty, over half of the SDRs would go to countries too rich to qualify for concessional aid from the IDA (Cline 1976, p. 63). Thus, questions about the efficiency of the link must be combined with concern about its appropriateness.

Inflation

If SDRs are created to supply the demand for world reserves, they need not be inflationary. But the need for reserves is poorly understood, and SDR emissions put forward under the current arrangements can only be considered approximations of reserve demand. A neutral allocation (i.e., in proportion to IMF quotas) may minimize mistakes of overallocation, since countries receiving too many SDRs simply will not use them. If SDRs were distributed disproportionately to LDCs, any overallocations would increase the world money supply, since the reason for such an allocation is to enable LDCs to spend them (Williamson 1977, p. 87).

In one sense, the question of how to distribute the SDRs is moot, since the current size of SDR emissions is too small to have much impact upon world inflation anyway (Cline 1976, pp. 86–87), but perceptions are important, and MDC representatives do not trust LDC governments to manage their money supplies so as to control world inflation. Indeed, one of the most frequent complaints of LDCs is that the IMF stabilization policy (considered essential by MDC representatives) is too harsh. Greater LDC control over the IMF and its activities would, in the words of a former head of West Germany's central bank, "be the death of [the] institution" (Janssen and Bacon 1980, p. 11). In general, MDC representatives believe that their LDC colleagues view SDRs as "free money." Should the LDCs have their way, the inflationary impact of SDRs would surely grow. Indeed, continual LDC lobbying for more SDRs during the 1970s, when world liquidity was in excess, tended to confirm this view.

Size of the Link

The amounts of SDR link aid would be small even if the link were put into effect. During the first allocation (1970–1972), 3 billion SDRs were issued per year, and three-fourths of them went to the MDCs. If one-half of the MDC allocation had gone to the LDCs via the link instead, the extra aid would have amounted to slightly more than $1 billion. Since concessional aid over the same period averaged about $8 billion, the extra aid would have amounted to a 12 percent increase, provided there had been no offsetting effect (Cline 1976, p. 59). Since it is unlikely that MDCs would maintain other aid flows at current levels if a link were put into effect, the net increment of aid would probably be much less.

The quality of link aid would also be low. Cline (1976, p. 60), has pointed out that the grant element in aid flowing from the Organization for Economic Cooperation and Development (OECD) countries in the early 1970s was about 80 percent. Since an interest charge of 5 percent is levied against SDRs actually used, the grant element in link aid would only be about 50 percent, when the same discount rate is used for comparison (10 percent). Thus, each dollar of link aid would be worth much less than a dollar of OECD-type aid. Cline has estimated (1976, p. 91) that the total LDC welfare gain from link aid would be in the neighborhood of only 1 percent above what is gained through normal trade and capital flows.

Future Emissions

Future emissions of SDRs in the medium to long run may be nil. The problem that SDRs were created to solve, a world liquidity shortage, has been largely solved by events of the 1970s. The collapse of the Bretton Woods system during the 1971–1973 period was accompanied by an enormous outflow of dollars as countries sought to stem speculation on dollar devaluation. Dollars flowed into the coffers of the monetary authorities in major OECD countries, and the monetary expansion caused by this reserve accumulation led (in part) to the inflation we see today. This inflation is an indication that the demand for reserves was less than the supply, so the excess supply has spilled over into inflationary monetary growth. Since SDRs are meant to increase reserves, the new conditions imply a decreased need for them.[6]

Reserves increased further after the oil price increases of 1974. OPEC surpluses after that date flowed largely into Eurocurrency markets, where funds are lent to deficit countries. Also, U.S. attempts to support the dollar during 1977 and 1979 meant another surge of liquidity on world markets.

At the same time that world reserves were expanding as never before, the demand for reserves was reduced by the breakup of the Bretton Woods system. Before 1971, countries had to buy and sell currencies to maintain pegged exchange rates, but floating exchange rates after 1971 (and particularly after March 1973) reduced the demand for reserves. Since the danger of a devaluation of reserve currencies was reduced after 1973, monetary authorities were more inclined to hold reserve currencies than SDRs. Since currency reserves earn interest and SDRs do not, a monetary authority would prefer currency *if* there were little danger of devaluation. Since that danger was reduced after 1973, the demand for SDRs as reserves declined.

It was probably a mistake that SDRs were issued at all in the late 1970s. The IMF Board of Governors chose to ignore the worldwide surplus liquidity and authorized an emission of about 4 billion SDRs per year from 1979 to 1981. The board reasoned that if SDRs were to become a central part of the reserve system, then at least a token amount would have to be issued—there was also some lobbying by LDCs for that action (Cline 1979, p. 343). Given world conditions and the liquidity role of SDRs, the move was ill-advised, and at the current time, no distribution of new SDRs is being considered seriously.

Conclusion

The question of an SDR link to aid is probably moot. Excess world liquidity precludes the issuance of additional SDRs in the near future and in any event, the aid component of an SDR link would be very small and probably inefficient. The world's LDLDCs would benefit little from a link proposal, even if SDRs were issued in greater proportion to them.

We see no reason for the link proposal to be pursued further. MCDs are unlikely to agree to any link so long as they perceive poor financial management among LDCs, and so long as they view the IMF as a major tool for solving their own monetary problems. Furthermore, the IMF has assumed a number of nontraditional roles to take care of special problems facing the LDCs. These include special facilities such as the Oil Facility, the Supplementary Financing Facility, and the Compensatory Facility (see Guru 1979). The main benefit that LDCs can expect from the IMF is a set of reforms to help cure the economic ills of the MDCs. Any conceivable benefits from an SDR-aid link are dwarfed by the benefits that would flow from a healthy recovery of MDC economies and an ensuing expansion of world trade. Intransigence on the link issue by LDCs simply postpones reform, without much changing its shape, and retards improvements for all countries.

Notes

1. All IMF members entered foreign exchange markets except the United States. Since all currencies were defined in terms of dollars, if the other IMF members acted to maintain the exchange rates, the United States did not need to do anything.

2. The Dillon round (1960–1961) and the Kennedy round (1964–1967) were both held under the auspices of the GATT.

3. At first, \$1 equaled 1 SDR. Now the SDR is pegged to a weighted average of the world's major currencies. The dollar depreciated, and by April 1982, \$1.13 equaled 1 SDR.

4. The committee's official name was Committee on Reform of the International Monetary System of the IMF Board of Governors.

5. The link proposal suggests a somewhat greater allocation to a selected list of LDLDCs. This allocation is not great enough to affect our general statements about SDR distribution, however.

6. For details, see Black (1978).

Bibliography

Black, S. W. "Policy Responses to Major Disturbances of the 1970s and Their Transmission Through International Goods and Capital Markets." *Weltwirtschaftliches Archiv* 114:4 (1978), 614–641.

Block, Fred L. *The Origins of International Economic Disorder.* Berkeley: University of California Press, 1977.

Cline, W. R. *International Monetary Reform and the Developing Countries.* Washington, D.C.: Brookings Institution, 1976.

_____ . "Resource Transfers to the Developing Countries: Issues and Trends."

In *Policy Alternatives for a New International Economic Order,* edited by W. R. Cline, pp. 330–353. New York: Praeger, 1979.

Erb, R. D. "International Resource Transfers: The International Financial System and Foreign Aid." In *Challenges to a Liberal International Economic Order,* edited by R. C. Amacher, G. Haberler, and T. D. Willett, pp. 383–420. Washington, D.C.: American Enterprise Institute, 1979.

Guru, D. D. "International Monetary System, Second Amendment, and Developing Countries." *Economic Affairs* 24:10–12 (October–December 1979), 231–240 and 273–276.

Janssen, R. F., and Bacon, K. H. "Carter Tells World Bank, IMF to Defend Roles in Setting Global Financial Policy." *Wall Street Journal,* October 1, 1980.

Scammell, W. M. *International Monetary Policy: Bretton Woods and After.* London: Macmillan, 1975.

Williamson, J. "SDRs: The Link." In *The New International Economic Order: The North-South Debate,* edited by J. Bhagwati, pp. 81–100. Cambridge, Mass.: MIT Press, 1977.

$$6$$

Debt

The NIEO plan calls for "debt renegotiation on a case-by-case basis with a view to concluding agreements on debt cancellation, moratorium, rescheduling, or interest subsidization" (II, 2, g). This call was a response to a growing international indebtedness on the part of the LDCs. Furthermore, since the time NIEO was declared in 1974, the international debt of LDCs has approximately doubled.

One must assume that NIEO is suggesting further concessions than those that have already been granted in the case-by-case negotiations of the Paris Club (see section on "Debt Rescheduling" late in this chapter). Both the popular and the scholarly literature offer few clues about the criteria for further concessions, however, and the diplomatic literature provides no generalizations. Therefore, we must proceed somewhat in the dark.

We will review LDC debt to try to perceive the dimensions of the problem, and we will find that not all debt is alike and, by the same token, different situations call for different actions. We will review the institutions that have been handling debt rescheduling, as well as the country cases since 1956. Finally, we will examine more closely the cases of three countries (Turkey, Peru, and Bolivia) that have borrowed heavily and have needed relief. Our general conclusion will be that current institutions of debt relief are up to the task and that no major institutional changes are required.

The international credit system is a delicate and essential element in world trade. Any changes in its structure should be made with care, so as not to dam up the smooth flow of credit. If debt cancellation or rescheduling should become routine, rather than infrequent, responses to emergency situations, we fear that a normal offering of credit may be impaired in the future.

Review of the Situation

External debt of LDCs grew almost fourfold from 1970 to 1977, and a further fivefold jump is expected before 1990 (see Table 6.1). In 1970,

TABLE 6.1
LDC Medium-and Long-term Debt Outstanding (Billion $)

	1970	1977	1985	1990
Total	68	258	740	1278
To Private Creditors	32	155	438	771
To Official Creditors	37	104	302	507
Total in $ of 1975	113	231	348	449

Source: World Bank, World Development Report 1979, New York: Oxford University Press, 1979, p. 29.

Note: Discrepancies in totals due to rounding.

outstanding debt was divided about equally between public and private creditors; since then, private sources have taken the lead. Private credits are not subsidized, while official credits sometimes are; therefore, this shift has been associated with a hardening of terms.

Some debt relief has been provided by inflation in MDCs, since repayments will be in currency that has a lower purchasing power than what was borrowed. The final line of Table 6.1 reveals that in constant prices, the debt expansion has not been nearly so precipitous as would appear when it is figured in current prices. From 1970 to 1977, real debt approximately doubled; if inflation in MDCs continues as predicted, the real debt of the LDCs is projected to grow annually at about 5.2 percent until 1990.

On the average, interest rates paid by LDCs on all external debts have been less than world inflation rates; hence, the average real rate is negative. Smith (1979) has calculated that the debt service burden was reduced by 36 percent from 1973 to 1976, compared to what it would have been if prices had remained stable. During 1973-1982, inflation has reduced the present value of the debt service far more than a total forgiveness of interest payments would have done had prices been stable (Smith 1979, p. 292).

Nevertheless, each country must live in the present, servicing today's debt with today's income. Hence, relief via inflation does not preclude problems.

Alternative Explanations of LDC Debt

Unfortunately, neither economists nor diplomats are agreed on why LDC debt has burgeoned. Three nonexclusive explanations are common:

1. Recession in MDCs may have reduced the export earnings of LDCs. To sustain imports necessary for their own growth, LDCs have had to borrow.
2. The terms of trade of LDCs have declined; again to sustain their imports, LDCs have had to borrow.
3. LDCs have had to borrow to finance the increase in oil prices since 1973.

First Explanation: Recession

In Chapter 3, we saw that LDC exports were generally sustained during the 1970s and that in some countries, they even grew. Although export growth occurred most heavily in NICs, most LDCs did share in it. We do not believe this experience was a reversal of the normal situation, in which LDC exports depend on the economic health of the MDCs; rather, the stagflation of the late seventies did not present a sufficiently severe recession to cause damage.

That judgment, however, does not preclude an argument that LDCs had been expecting import expansion over and above what could be financed through export proceeds, so that the latter might have increased by more had MDCs been in better economic health. Alternatively, LDCs may borrow to take advantage of profitable investment opportunities that require financing in excess of current export earnings, but the "cause" of the debt then shifts to the internal decision to expand imports.

Second Explanation: Terms of Trade

The second explanation (terms of trade) can be distinguished from the third (oil prices) only if we segregate the terms of trade of LDCs vis-à-vis MDCs. Using data from the United Nations and the International Monetary Fund, we showed in Chapter 2 that there has been no net deterioration in the terms of trade of NOPECs vis-à-vis MDCs during the postwar period. Declining terms of trade in some subperiods are offset by rising terms in others. Consequently, apart from oil, it is hard to explain the increasing debt in terms of increasing import prices.

Third Explanation: Increase in Price of Oil

Clearly, the increased price of oil after 1973 has much to do with NOPECs' indebtedness. If it were the prime cause, however, we would expect the rate of increase in NOPEC indebtedness to have increased after 1973, but it did not (World Bank 1979a, p. 28). Katz (1979, p. 4) shows that in real terms, the NOPEC debt expanded by 15.5 percent annually from 1967 to 1973 but only by 11.9 percent from 1973 to 1977.[1] The same pattern holds whether the debt is from private or official sources.

The usual reasons for the debt problem, therefore, tell us little. Why? Probably because they were deduced "in the aggregate" by looking at the overall situation without paying sufficient attention to the idiosyncracies of different countries. So, we will now look at some individual cases, and we have tried to group countries according to common characteristics. The most useful grouping is probably by per capita income.

The Pattern of LDC Borrowing

Commercial borrowing by middle-income countries accounts for 79 percent of the LDC debt outstanding at the end of 1978. Of this, 45 percent was owed by only seven countries.[2] These countries generally have strong export sectors—particularly manufacturing exports—and substantial reserves. These same countries also account for almost all of the private debt as only 6 percent of the private debt is owed by low-income LDCs.

Table 6.2 lists the rank order of the ten top debtor countries for each of four dimensions: total debt, official debt, private debt, and debt service. Not only does this list of sixteen countries account for most of the debt "problem," but it contains almost the same set of countries identified in Chaper 3 as the newly industrializing countries.

Some countries in Table 6.2 are distinguished from the others by special circumstances. Four of them are oil exporters (Indonesia, Algeria, Iran, and Venezuela). Surely the high price of oil cannot be a reason for their debt! The World Bank (1979b, pp 13–15) classifies Spain and Israel as high-income developing countries, while Argentina, Yugoslavia, and Iran belong to the "upper-middle" income group. Per capita income in all the above countries exceeds $2,000. If high-income and oil-exporting countries are removed from the "problem," only eight remain: Brazil, Chile, South Korea, Mexico, and Turkey (all middle income), plus Egypt, India, and Pakistan (low income). No sub-Saharan African countries are in the group.

Egypt, India, Indonesia, and Pakistan are the poorest countries listed in Table 6.2. They have been able to borrow a great deal because they qualify for concessional assistance. They are very poor and very large; they are also politically important. In *official* debt ranking, they hold

TABLE 6.2
Principal Debtor Countries, 1978 (rankings)

Country	Per Capita Income (1978)	Disbursed Debt Outstanding			Debt Service
		Total	Official Sources	Private Sources	
Algeria	1260	6	*	4	8
Argentina	2767	*	*	7	4
Brazil	1570	1	7	1	1
Chile	1410	*	*	*	10
Egypt	390	*	2	*	*
India	180	3	1	*	*
Indonesia	360	4	3	10	6
Iran	2160	9	*	6	7
Israel	3500	8	5	*	*
Korea, South	1160	7	8	8	5
Mexico	1290	2	9	2	2
Pakistan	230	*	4	*	*
Spain	3470	5	*	3	3
Turkey	1200	*	6	*	*
Venezuela	2910	*	*	5	*
Yugoslavia	2380	10	10	9	9
Ten largest as percent of total		54.8	54.0	68.3	60.1

Source: World Bank, World Development Report 1980, New York: Oxford University Press, 1980; World Bank, World Debt Tables, vol. 1, Washington, D.C., December 1979, various tables.

*Not one of the ten largest.

the first four places, but India, Egypt, and Pakistan do not even rank in the first ten in private debt or in debt service. Indonesia is able to rank tenth in loans from private sources only because of petroleum-related activity, which has engendered a development boom of late.

Our disaggregated look at the principal potential beneficiaries of debt forgiveness, and their relative wealth among LDCs, does not readily persuade us of the equity of this NIEO proposal. Since debt forgiveness is essentially foreign aid, we wonder whether the same resources might not be directed instead to the more needy recipients.

How Severe Is the Debt Burden?

Two measures are normally used to judge the severity of debt burden: the maturity structure (or rate of amortization) and the debt service ratio (ratio of principal and interest payments to exports over a given time period, usually one year). Table 6.3 presents the former, and Table 6.4 the latter. Table 6.3 also includes amounts of indebtedness, average interest rates, and the percent of grant element for 1972 to 1978.[3]

In general, terms hardened during the seventies. Interest rates rose for both official and private loans, though maturities remained about the same. Private loans tended to be for a shorter term (8.9 years in 1978) than official loans (24.8 years). In both cases, however, terms in 1978 were a bit softer than in 1976, when interest rates peaked and maturities were at their shortest for all loan categories.

Official lenders divide into international organizations and governments. Loans from the former increased more from 1972 to 1978 than loans from the latter (24 percent per year average compared to a bit over 9 percent). Furthermore, interest rates set by international organizations were slightly lower in 1978 than in 1972; hence, the grant element in their loans stayed about the same.

In contrast to the maturity structure, the debt service ratio indicates a country's liquidity position—how capable it is of servicing its debt at a given time. But debt service may fluctuate widely because of prepayments, late payments, or refinancing (World Bank 1979a). Export revenues reflect changes in international markets and even in the weather (for crop exports). Thus, the debt service ratio of a given year may not be representative; it may reflect momentary liquidity rather than overall economic health.

Table 6.4 shows the ratios for low- and middle-income countries. An increasing use of loans from private sources hardened the terms for middle-income countries, thus their debt service ratio rose during the seventies. Low-income countries, on the other hand, continued to obtain concessional loans, so their 1977 ratio fell below the 1970 level. Katz

TABLE 6.3
Average Terms of Loan Commitments of Official and Private Creditors, 1972-78 (Billions of $)

	1972	1975	1977	1978
Total Official Lenders				
Amount	11.6	21.9	25.8	27.2
Interest rate (%)	4.3	4.9	5.2	5.0
Maturity (years)	24.2	23.5	22.6	24.8
Grant element (%)	39.9	36.1	33.9	37.0
Government Lenders				
Amount	7.9	13.8	13.5	13.4
Interest rate (%)	3.8	4.2	4.4	4.7
Maturity (years)	22.7	21.1	22.5	23.9
Grant element (%)	42.6	39.2	38.0	38.7
International Organizations				
Amount	3.8	8.1	12.3	13.8
Interest rate (%)	5.5	6.1	5.9	5.2
Maturity (years)	27.5	27.7	22.9	25.7
Grant element (%)	34.2	31.0	29.4	35.4
Total Private Lenders				
Amount	8.8	23.8	37.0	49.8
Interest rate (%)	7.3	8.8	8.0	9.4
Maturity (years)	8.9	7.8	8.0	8.9
Grant element (%)	10.9	4.7	7.0	1.7

Source: World Bank, World Debt Tables, vol. 2, p. 194.

Note: Discrepancies in totals due to rounding.

TABLE 6.4
Debt Service Ratios

	1970	1975	1976	1977
Low Income Countries	13.7	11.8	12.3	12.6
Middle Income Countries	10.2	10.3	10.1	11.8
All LDCs	10.6	10.5	10.3	11.8

Source: Katz, 1979, p. 29.

(1979, p. 15) places 71 percent of the official, concessional loans in low-income countries in 1977.

In both cases, the surprising factor is that the ratios have not changed very much, and the reason for that is that the rapid rise of exports (denominator) have increased the countries' debt service ability (numerator). Indeed, the slight rise for all LDCs is probably attributable to the accelerated borrowing of a few countries.

In Table 6.5, we again disaggregate the data and return to the country listing of Table 6.2. Now, however, the countries are rearranged according to whether they are low income, high income, or others. The low-income countries improved their positions during the seventies, probably because of the sustained grant element plus an expansion in international-organization credits. The middle-income group was more diversified. Chile's ratio jumped startlingly because of both increased debt and poor export performance. Brazil (the heaviest debtor of all LDCs) and Mexico have among the highest ratios in the world. The governments of both countries have actively pursued foreign loans as a means to rapid development, which they believe will cover the debt service and leave them better off eventually. LDC diplomats pressing for debt relief usually find little support from Brazil and Mexico, as those governments are more concerned about their credit ratings for future borrowing than they are about forgiveness of the present debt. Turkey's debt service ratio declined because of rescheduling, and South Korea's ratio fell because of rapid export growth despite large amounts of debt outstanding.

Of the other countries, some show increasing ratios, others decreasing. Three of the four oil-exporting countries (Algeria, Indonesia, and Venezuela) had higher ratios in 1978 than in 1970. Argentina's high and growing ratio occurred because of slow growth and slow export expansion—and Argentina has been a heavy debtor for many years.

TABLE 6.5
Debt Service Ratios of Principal Debtor Countries

	1970	1978
Low Income		
Egypt	28.7	22.2
India	20.9	9.4
Pakistan	21.6	12.2
Middle Income		
Brazil	13.5	28.4
Chile	18.9	38.2
Korea, South	19.4	10.5
Mexico	23.6	59.6
Turkey	16.3	11.0
Others		
Algeria	3.2	20.9
Argentina	21.5	26.8
Indonesia	6.9	13.0
Iran	12.2	3.2[a]
Israel	12.3	8.1
Spain	3.6	11.0
Venezuela	2.9	6.9
Yugoslavia	8.2	3.2

Source: World Bank, World Development Report 1980 and 1979.

[a] 1977

Israel and Yugoslavia, whose ratios have been decreasing, along with Spain, may well be considered MDCs.

An Interim Assessment

Although oil prices are surely a factor in LDC indebtedness, much of the growth of the debt has also been due to a desire to import for investment purposes. However, aggregate data can hide the facts of individual-country borrowing. Most of the debt increase has occurred in a relatively small group of middle- and upper-income LDCs. Although the world's poorest countries have indeed been borrowing, their relative debt burdens have not changed much. Terms for higher-income countries have hardened as they have turned more to private sources to obtain loans.

Experiences vary widely among countries. Some of the heaviest borrowers on the hardest terms do not have "problems." For some of them, exports have expanded as planned, so the debt service has become lighter. Other borrowers (such as Mexico and Brazil) see the debt burden as being temporarily high while local productive capacity is being built up. Some people view debt cancellations or rescheduling as harbingers of harder terms for future LDC borrowing, and some research has shown that LDCs actually benefit from rules that *increase* penalties for default (Eaton and Gersovitz 1981). Sometimes the debt problem stems from external forces (such as a market slump), but just as often, it arises because of internal problems (such as over-ambitious public spending). Even the fact that a country has oil revenues does not guarantee lower debt burdens (for example, Indonesia, Venezuela, and Algeria have increasing debt service ratios).

Because each country's experience is different, it is difficult to generalize about debt problems. NIEO does not ask for blanket forgiveness or rescheduling, suggesting case-by-case treatment instead, but isn't case-by-case treatment already being done satisfactorily? Is there a need for a new international arrangement? To answer these questions, let us now turn to the ways in which debt relief currently occurs on a case-by-case basis.

Debt Relief for LDCs

Debt Cancellation

Some MDCs have already canceled debts owed by the poorest countries. Canada, Sweden, and Switzerland were the first MDCs to do so; the United Kingdom followed suit shortly thereafter. West Germany has selectively canceled debts of $2.3 billion, and Japan $1.2 billion (MacBean 1980). The total forgiveness—about $6.2 billion—is not large compared to the world debt that is outstanding, but it has been particularly helpful to the poorest countries. In each case, cancellation immediately releases foreign exchange that otherwise would have gone to debt service.

But the initial wave of cancellations has ebbed. Other MDC governments point out that official loans already contain a grant element. Further cancellation would increase foreign aid, which is a matter of legislative policy within aid-donor countries.

Debt Rescheduling

Rescheduling—the avenue of relief for most middle-income countries— occurs when payments difficulties arise and countries run the risk of bankruptcy because of a shortage of reserves. Most rescheduling negotiations occur through an informal, ad hoc group of creditor countries known as "the Paris Club" (named after the most popular city for negotiations). The "membership" of the Paris Club varies with each case, and it was first convened in 1956 to facilitate a multilateral settlement with Argentina. Occasionally, multinational negotiations occur under other auspices, such as OECD or a World Bank consortium.

Debt rescheduling was necessary for twelve countries from 1956 to 1978 (see Table 6.6), and in 1980–1981, rescheduling attempts were undertaken by Turkey, Peru, Zaire, Bolivia, the Sudan, Nicaragua, and Jamaica. Suppliers' credits have been the principal kind of debt to be rescheduled. These loans tend to have maturities that are determined more by the phasing of projects rather than by debt service considerations; if the maturities bunch up, a temporary problem is created. Consolidation with longer maturity is the answer.

During the seventies, however, other kinds of reschedulings became common. India's debts—including all public debts—were rescheduled several times. The secession of Bangladesh in 1971 necessitated a rescheduling of all medium- and long-term debts for Pakistan. Sometimes rescheduling is necessary to correct severe mismanagement. The Sukarno regime in Indonesia incurred extreme budget deficits in its last years, largely for consumption, and left a legacy of $2.3 billion of debt (Abbot 1979, p. 227). As a result, all public debts had to be rescheduled between 1966 and 1970. A similar situation faced Chile in the early and mid-seventies.

In most cases, the need to reschedule arises because of a combination of adverse circumstances that affect foreign exchange earnings. Large investment programs, deficit financing, and exchange controls often lead to these difficulties. In Turkey, for example, expansionist policies were

TABLE 6.6
Multilateral Debt Renegotiations for Developing Countries
Between 1956 and 1978

Country	Year	Country	Year
Argentina	1956	Indonesia	1966
	1962		1967
	1965		1968
			1970
Brazil	1961		
	1964	Pakistan	1972
			1973
Cambodia	1972[a]		1974
(now Kampuchea)			
		Peru	1968
Chile	1965		1969
	1972		1978
	1974		
	1975	Sierra Leone	1977
Ghana	1966	Turkey	1959
	1968		1965
	1970		1978
	1974		
		Zaire	1976
India	1968		1977
	1971		
	1972		
	1973		
	1974		
	1975		
	1976		
	1977		
	1978		

Source: Albert C. Cizaukas, "International Debt Renegotiation," World Development, Vol. 7, 1979, p. 209, fn 17.

[a]Cambodia (1972) involved two separate agreements, one in
January and one in November.

based on the belief that the favorable circumstances of the fifties would
continue, but they did not.

Fluctuations in export prices have also brought about rescheduling,
despite the fact that the International Monetary Fund has a special
facility for these cases. Adverse cocoa prices affected Ghana, and low
coffee and copper prices affected Brazil and Chile, respectively. In virtually
all cases, poor management combined with bad luck.

Our endorsement of the Paris Club—rather than any new arrangement—stems from the fact that it is working well and we see no need to expand rescheduling beyond the kinds of cases already being treated. Each country is free to make its own case before its creditors. Creditors have been realistic, since they understand it is not to their advantage to drive a debtor country into bankruptcy. The Paris Club is flexible enough to distinguish between cases of mismanagement and those caused by unusual circumstances, such as natural disasters, and the form of relief can fit the circumstances.

Some Country Cases

A few LDCs have serious debt problems, and the cause is usually domestic mismanagement that was allowed to continue because international markets were favorable. As soon as the international situation became adverse, the problem surfaced—and, of course, the international situation rather than the mismanagement has been blamed. Three such countries are Turkey, Peru, and Bolivia.

Turkey

Turkey has rescheduled its debt three times—in 1959, 1965, and 1978. Expansionary policies in the 1950s, combined with a decline in export proceeds, led the government to impose tight controls on trade and payments. By 1950, the lira was severely overvalued, and the country was almost bankrupt. Turkey's creditors agreed to rescheduling in 1959 only after the government had committed itself to a major devaluation and stabilization program. Unfortunately, Turkish policymakers treated this program as a one-time-only maneuver. They quickly slipped back to establishing price and exchange controls, and by 1965, the conditions of the late 1950s had recurred. The second rescheduling included many debts that had already been rescheduled in 1959.

Price and exchange controls and restrictions on trade all reappeared during the 1970s, despite their failures in the 1950s and 1960s. The balance of payments had become heavily dependent upon remittances from Turkish workers in the EEC, and that foreign exchange inflow allowed an import substitution policy without the foreign exchange constraints such a policy normally engenders. Import substitution industries were "subsidized" through exchange and credit controls and other barriers to competition. Most countries have found that this process quickly leads to production inefficiencies and a balance-of-payments deficit stemming from the intermediate and capital imports required by the new industry.

The favorable international situation was reversed in the mid-1970s. A recession in Europe sent many Turkish workers home, and remittances fell sharply. Simultaneously, oil price increases greatly strained Turkey's current account. By 1977, Turkey had the highest ratio of oil imports to goods exports in the world: 79 percent.

Rather than using policies that would help adjustment to the new conditions, Turkish officials resorted to even tighter controls. Funds borrowed on a short-term basis covered the import needs of the inefficient import substitution industries. Overall growth rates declined after 1975, and most industries began to operate far below capacity. As controls became more strict, increasing numbers of transactions were carried on in the black market.

By 1978, Turkey again had a serious debt problem. Foreign exchange earnings were estimated to be approximately $3 billion ($2 billion from exports; $1 billion from remittances). Debt service payments were about $500 million on long-term loans and $5.1 billion on short-term credits (*Economist* September 13, 1980, p. 97). "Normal" imports for that year would have been about $5 billion. Thus, Turkey required a capital inflow of $7.6 billion, and the only place where it could be obtained was, once again, the short-term credit market. Debt reschedulings in 1978 and 1979 were designed to convert short-term to long-term debt.

Peru

Peru rescheduled its debt in 1968, 1969, and 1978. In both periods, the difficulty stemmed from large budget deficits and extreme misman-agement. Upon taking office in 1963, the Belaúnde government attempted to expand the economic base of the country through a number of public investment projects. The government deficit increased from 7.3 percent of revenues in 1963 to over 27 percent in 1967. Most of this deficit was financed by foreign borrowing; domestic credit increased at over 20 percent per year, and inflation and the balance of payments were kept within bounds by price and exchange controls. By 1968, the debt burden had become unmanageable because of shrunken export proceeds. Inflation, bottled up by price controls, was taking its toll on economic efficiency. When the Belaúnde government was overthrown in 1968, debt renegotiations took place.

Ten years later, Peru had a similar problem for similar reasons, but by that time, most of the creditors were private (Dhonte 1979, pp. 3–23). In the early 1970s, oil had been discovered in the upper Amazon basin, and there had been talk of a "new Saudi Arabia." Peru was able to borrow heavily in private capital markets on the promise that oil revenues would provide the means for repayment. Publicly borrowed funds were committed to major development projects. Spending on military equipment was a top priority. Despite an annual growth of credit in excess of 40 percent (1974-1977), inflation was held in check by price controls, and there were few devaluations of the sol.

By 1978, the public sector's deficit hit 11 percent of gross domestic product (GDP), the country had run out of credit, and the government was unable to honor a standby agreement with the IMF that had been signed in October 1977. Peru's international reserves were overdrawn by $1.3 billion, and public-sector debt (as well as private debt) was in technical default (*Euromoney* June 1980, pp. 16-18). In general, there was a consensus that "economic management in Lima was abysmal" (*Economist* March 22, 1980).

Since rescheduling its debt in 1978, Peru has paid a heavy price for the mismanagement of the 1970s. Prices freed from controls increased at over 70 percent per year, strikes and unrest became widespread, and the real income of Peruvians fell by about 40 percent in 1979. Current policy is aimed at public austerity, trade liberalization, and freeing internal controls. Estimates are that a recovery began in 1980 (*Euromoney* June 1980, pp. 16-18) though only time will tell whether Peru's management is on a firmer base.

Bolivia

Bolivia's recent economic problems may require debt rescheduling even though shifts in the international economy have so far been favorable for Bolivia. The prices of minerals and oil, Bolivia's main exports, have risen sharply, and from 1973 through 1977, the GDP grew at 6 percent per year in real terms. Public spending, however, has been more ambitious than even the expanding economy could sustain, and at times since the mid-1970s, the government deficit has exceeded 10 percent of GDP. Although most of this deficit was covered by borrowing internationally, some of it simply spilled over into domestic inflation.

Estimates put Bolivia's total external debt at $3.4 billion at the end of 1979. Debt service for that year was 32 percent of export earnings, and it was estimated that it would rise to 40 percent in 1980 (*Euromoney* April 1980, p. 80). Part of Bolivia's problem is that export revenues did not rise as expected. The production of minerals has stagnated, and that of petroleum has declined since 1973. International reserves have withered, and current-account deficits have grown. In 1980, the Bolivian government was forced into a standby arrangement with the IMF to cover its foreign exchange requirements, and concern is now widely felt that the country may have to reschedule its debt should current trends continue. As a London banker has put it (*Euromoney* April 1980, p. 80), "it is hard to assess [Bolivia's situation]. The continuity of IMF involvement is essential."

Conclusion

Countries do indeed encounter debt problems. However, the debt problem of many countries is not as great as has been assumed. Inflation makes debt *appear* to grow rapidly, but as long as export revenues increase apace, no debt service problem need arise. Oil price increases are presumed to be the primary cause of current debt problems, yet LDC debt increased more rapidly before 1973 than afterward. The main reason for debt increases is that governments have chosen to borrow. Most often that borrowing has allowed them to make investments that otherwise would not have been possible. Where those investments have been sound, the payoff from them has allowed the countries to make their debt-service payments with little or no difficulty.

Most LDC governments manage their debts well; the few extreme problem cases arise mainly from mismanagement. Overly ambitious public expenditure programs, combined with price, trade, and exchange controls create conditions for poor economic performance. When combined with borrowing to finance current spending, a debt problem becomes almost inevitable.

No across-the-board international debt rescheduling program seems called for. Some LDC governments even oppose debt forgiveness, which they think would slow the flow of credit to those of them who do use it well. Furthermore, general debt rescheduling or forgiveness would benefit mainly high-income LDCs, which do not have severe debt problems.

The few problem cases are specific to the countries and lenders concerned and are not generally the result of world conditions. It would appear that the Paris Club and other ad hoc arrangements provide an adequate opportunity for both borrowers and lenders to work out debt management plans that suit the interests of both.[4]

Notes

1. In current dollars, total debt grew at about the same rate in 1967-1973 (20.0 percent) as in 1973-1977 (20.5 percent).

2. Brazil, Mexico, India, Indonesia, Spain, Algeria, and South Korea.

3. The grant element on concessional loans is the difference between the loan service (amortization and interest) that would have to be paid under market conditions and the loan service at concessional rates, calculated in present discounted values.

4. Since Chapter 6 was written, a world financial crisis has emerged, associated

primarily with Mexico, but also with Brazil and with eastern Europe as a group, plus some less influential areas. This crisis does not change the main thrust of Chapter 6, the reasons for this being explained in the appendix below.

APPENDIX

(written September 10, 1982)

As this volume goes to press, a world financial crisis has emerged from the inability of Mexico to meet its foreign obligations, as well as from precarious financial conditions in Brazil, Poland, Costa Rica, Pakistan, and a few other countries (see Bergsten in the *New York Times*, Aug. 26, 1982).* Mexico's crisis is being met by a $1.85 billion package of loans put together through the U.S. Federal Reserve Board, the Bank of International Settlements, and the central banks of eleven countries, provided that Mexico adheres to austerity measures determined by the International Monetary Fund (see Lewis in the *New York Times*, Aug. 31, 1982).† Similar arrangements may be worked out for other countries if and when their crises boil. The resources of the International Monetary Fund will probably be expanded to enhance its future capabilities to meet similar cases.

The Mexican crisis arises out of government commitments to vast public expenditures from projected oil revenue that did not materialize. (Peru's financial crisis a few years ago had a similar origin.) To relieve the political pressure, the president of Mexico promptly nationalized the banks. To us, this is like shooting the messenger who brings news of military defeat. It is also curious how an overly centralized power structure can use its own failures further to enhance its power.

Nothing in this experience calls for a routine system of reducing or rescheduling debts. Like individuals, LDC governments must learn not to pre-spend expected bonanzas, a lesson that would easily be evaded under NIEO. The international financial system is capable of *exceptional* measures to prevent its own collapse, but it is important that they remain exceptional.

We do recognize an injustice in world powers rescuing a country (Mexico) so strong that its collapse would harm the international financial system, while abandoning another (Chile under Allende) of lesser importance. The different politics of these countries was also crucial. The similarities lie in the fact that disastrous economic policies, *not* foreign intervention, brought on both crises. Thus, weak countries with "incorrect" politics must be all the more vigilant for sound economic and financial structures than strong ones with "correct" politics. Yet the former group, forced to learn the need for soundness, may be the winners over the long haul.

* C. Fred Bergsten. "World Financial Crisis." *New York Times*, August 26, 1982.
† Lewis, Paul. "Mexico to Receive $1.85 Billion in Loans." *New York Times*, August 31, 1982.

Bibliography

Abbot, G. C. *International Indebtedness and the Developing Countries.* London: Croom Helm, 1979.

Cizuakas, A. C. "International Debt Renegotiation." *World Development* 7 (February 1979), 199–210.

Dhonte, P. *Clockwork Debt: Trade and the External Debt of Developing Countries.* Lexington, Mass.: Lexington Books, 1979.

Eaton, J., and Gersovitz, M. "Debt with Potential Repudiation: Theoretical and Empirical Analysis." *Review of Economic Studies* 48 (1981), 289–309.

7
Oil, Debt, Trade, and Growth

The LDC governments have been curiously uncomplaining about the price of oil—at least in public. Yet these increases have affected them, in proportion to their gross national product (GNP), far more adversely than they have the MDCs for the following reason.

Although both MDCs and NOPECs pay higher prices for oil, OPEC uses the proceeds primarily to buy goods in, or invest in, MDCs. The leftover proceeds are generally banked in MDCs. Thus, the net flow of money is from NOPECs, via OPEC, to MDCs. Doubtless, the lack of complaint by NOPECs comes from their political identification with OPEC. OPEC and NOPEC nations alike are LDCs, and NOPECs would like to imitate OPEC with respect to other export products. They seek an informal political liaison in their quest for NIEO.

Often, OPEC is credited with giving substantial aid to LDCs, which is usually quoted as a percentage of GNP: 1.38 percent in 1979, compared to 0.20 percent for the United States and 0.35 percent for all the (industrialized) countries that are a part of the Development Assistance Committee (OECD 1980, p. 101). However, more than 50 percent of OPEC's aid in 1979 went to two countries, Syria and Jordan, and most of the rest was paid to members of the Arab League, other Muslim countries, and India (see Table 7.1). OPEC is like the family that boasted of giving a substantial portion of its income in scholarships to worthy students, when in reality it was sending its own children to college. Very little OPEC aid goes to needy, non-Muslim countries in Africa.

In the present chapter, we discuss this situation in more depth and then ask, How do NOPECs adjust to the increased price of oil? To answer that question, we analyze the Latin American NOPECs, and we conclude that despite the serious negative consequences, most countries are adjusting quite well. For those that are not, the reasons do not relate primarily to oil, but to a mismanagement of resources in other

TABLE 7.1
Geographic Distribution of Aid from OPEC Countries and OPEC-Financed Multilateral Institutions, 1979

	Bilateral $ million	Multilateral $ million	Total $ million	% of Total
Syria	1,272.6	9.8	1,282.4	30.0
Jordan	878.4	9.3	887.7	20.8
Sudan	290.8	15.9	306.7	7.2
Arab Regional	257.3	–	257.3	6.0
Yemen A. R.	115.0	12.2	127.2	3.0
Somalia	75.9	10.6	86.5	2.0
Oman	76.5	0.2	76.7	1.8
Egypt	32.4	42.1	74.5	1.7
Mauritania	55.7	0.2	55.9	1.3
Pakistan	42.1	4.9	47.0	1.1
India	45.0	–	45.0	1.1
Bangladesh	13.3	10.5	23.8	0.6
Other Countries	533.8	137.2	671.0	15.6
Non-Arab Unallocated	331.3	–	331.3	7.8
Total	4,020.1	252.9	4,273.0	100.0
Contributions to World-wide Multilateral Institutions				
World Bank Group			425.8	64.3
International Fund for Arab Development			75.9	11.5
UN Development Program			9.1	1.4
Other UN			42.1	6.4
Regional Development Banks			37.1	5.6
Other			71.8	10.8
Total			661.8	100.0

Source: OECD, Development Cooperation: 1980 Review, Paris, 1980.

Note: Discrepancies in totals due to rounding.

ways. Loans to NOPECs are necessary to help them spread the adjustment over a number of years.

This chapter does not deal with NIEO directly. It does, however, illustrate some of the adjustments that will face LDCs that do not export primary products if the NIEO is successful in raising the prices of exports of the better-endowed LDCs. As only a few LDCs export any given primary product, only they will benefit if prices of those products rise. These LDCs are already the richest of the developing countries. All other LDCs would have to pay more and consume less.

Relative Impacts of Oil Price Increases[1]

Let us distinguish two separate balance-of-payments effects: the financial and the real. Financial effects refer to money balances, real effects to goods and services. MDCs may suffer strong real effects (paying more exports for a given amount of oil imports) but weak financial effects (if the money is returned to them for exports or investment). LDCs, however, have suffered strong financial as well as real effects. As a result, they have had to borrow heavily from MDCs. The summary picture is presented in Figures 7.1 and 7.2.

Each of these figures divides the world into four parts: OPEC, NOPEC Arab, NOPEC non-Arab, and industrialized countries. The arrows in Figure 7.1 express the difference in balance-of-payments categories between 1975 and 1970, and those in Figure 7.2 show the differences between 1978 and 1971.[2]

Subject to a warning for "roughness" (general orders of magnitudes only), the picture on real changes appears somewhat as follows. In 1975, industrialized countries paid $62.8 billion more for oil imports than they did in 1970; the 1978/1971 comparison is $84.4 billion. OPEC returned $34.9 billion of this excess to industrialized countries in 1975 by buying more goods and services, and $72.9 billion in 1978. Thus OPEC purchases from MDCs were creeping up, tending more and more to alleviate their balance of payments.

For non-Arab NOPECs, however, the picture is different. There was a significant increase in oil payments ($11.4 billion, 1975/1970, and $24.1 billion, 1978/1971). Aid from OPEC countries to NOPECs was negligible, by comparison.

The financial difference is measured by changes in reserves for MDCs and changes in reserves plus financial investment flows for non-Arab NOPECs. The 1975/1970 comparison shows that OPEC increased its financial reserves (on deposit or in short-term investments) in industrialized countries by $16.3 billion, and the long-term investment comparison is $4.2 billion (from OPEC to industrialized countries). In the

126

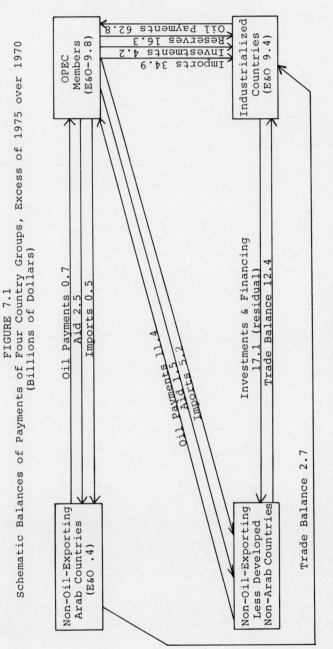

FIGURE 7.1

Schematic Balances of Payments of Four Country Groups, Excess of 1975 over 1970
(Billions of Dollars)

Arrows show direction of payments: imported goods flow in opposite direction.
E & O = errors and omissions.
Source: IMF, International Financial Statistics and Direction of Trade. Additional data from
OECD, Development Cooperation, 1976, p. 117. This figure was originally published in Powelson,
1977; the underlying balance of payments statements, country by country, were published in that
article and are not repeated here.

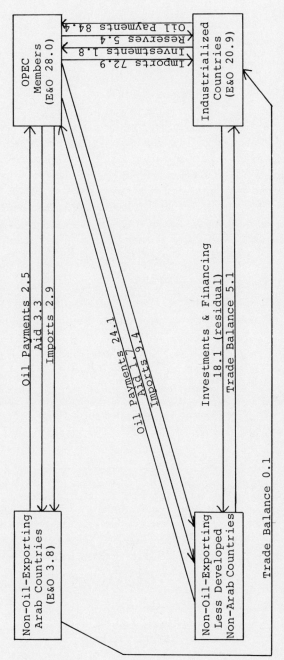

127

FIGURE 7.2

Schematic Balances of Payments of Four Country Groups, Excess of 1978 over 1971
(Billions of Dollars)

Arrows show direction of payments: imported goods flow in opposite direction. Investments and financing (industrialized to non-oil LDCs) is here calculated as residual for non-oil LDCs (hence zero errors and omissions). Errors and omissions (E&O) for all other areas are residuals, representing transactions with third countries and international institutions, as well as E&O in the original balance-of-payments statements.

Source: IMF, Balance of Payments Yearbook, Vol. 30, 1979; and IMF, Direction of Trade, Annual, 1972–78 and 1971–72. Additional data from OECD, Development Cooperation, 1980, p. 129. This figure was originally published in Powelson, 1981; the underlying balance of payments statements, country by country, were published in that article and are not repeated here.

1978/1971 comparison, OPEC's reserves were actually lower ($5.4 billion), because of a tapering off in the export of oil combined with increased imports. Investment had changed directions and flowed from industrialized countries to OPEC ($1.8 billion).

The changes for non-Arab NOPECs are measured by residuals, which are estimated to include both reductions in their reserves and borrowing from MDCs. In the 1975/1970 comparison, the residual figure was $17.1 billion, and in the 1978/1971 comparison, it was $18.1 billion.

None of these comparisons should be presumed to be caused entirely by the price of oil. Changes in the quantities of oil purchased, as a result of expanding GNP as well as policy decisions, were also causes. However, the Organization for Economic Cooperation and Development (OECD) has estimated the impact of the second round of oil price increases (1979 and 1980) on NOPECs, and it believes that the same volume of NOPEC oil imports for 1978 would have cost, in 1980 prices, $67.5 billion instead of $31.7 billion, or an increase of 113 percent. The percentage of GNP needed for oil imports rose from 2.9 to 5.2 percent (OECD 1980, p. 79).

The impact on NOPECs becomes the more severe when indirect effects are counted. Not all LDCs have their own refineries, so to a large extent, their purchases of petroleum products are not made directly from OPEC countries. For example, petrochemical products (e.g., fertilizers) are supplied largely by the industrialized nations. Indirectly, therefore, part of the $62.8 billion paid by the industrialized countries to OPEC nations in 1970–1975 was for oil that was eventually utilized in NOPECs. We have not estimated how much this part would be, but the trade balances of NOPECs with industrialized nations deteriorated by $12.4 billion (1975/1970) or $5.1 billion (1978/1971).

Balance-of-Payments Adjustment[3]

Sharply increased petroleum prices have an immediate and negative impact upon the current account (goods and services) of oil-importing countries. Such negative movements can usually be offset by devaluations in the exchange rate. In the case of oil, however, the problem is complex, for the price elasticity of demand is notoriously low. By increasing the cost of oil in local currency, devaluation or flexible exchange rates would most likely add to domestic inflation (Cohen 1978).

Let us enumerate, in general terms, the kinds of adjustments that could offset the negative impact of oil price increases.

1. The economy could contract. Since the problem is one of imports exceeding exports, a contraction of non-oil imports, caused by a contracting overall economy, could correct the imbalance at the expense of unemployment (Bird 1978).
2. The country might borrow to pay the higher prices.
3. Exports might be increased, and the proceeds used to pay the higher price of oil imports.
4. Dependency upon imported oil could be reduced, but only after a time lag.
5. Increased import barriers could reduce non-oil imports. (We will not analyze this possibility because trade restrictions for balance-of-payments adjustment are explicitly prohibited by the General Agreement on Tariffs and Trade {GATT}. Furthermore, Latin America has been moving away from import restrictions in the 1970s.)

Each of the first four adjustments—contraction, finance, export expansion, and reduced oil imports—requires a different time frame. In the very short run, a balance-of-payments deficit leads to economic contraction unless offset by policy measures, but this method is undesirable because of the decline in employment and income.

More time is normally required to arrange financing or to expand exports. Financing permits current expenditures to be sustained despite a balance-of-payments deficit, postponing the day of reckoning. If financing permits countries to continue stable economic growth, however, it could prove "costless," because income would rise to a point that is adequate for debt service. National income might then be higher than it would have been had there been no borrowing. This option depends on interest rates as well as on the productivity of borrowed capital.

Increased exports clearly require that the economy increase its productivity in relation to the rest of the world. This increase may require investment, with its "normal" gestation period, plus changes in monetary policy, trade agreements, and the like.

Oil imports could be reduced, in the short run, through import quotas and, over a longer period, through conservation, more energy-efficient investments, shifts toward nonenergy-intensive production, and so forth. Import quotas are likely to engender some losses in economic efficiency, but that would depend upon the administrative capabilities of the country concerned. In the long run, conservation will occur in response to higher prices. Since a large part of conservation requires replacing existing capital equipment with more energy-efficient equipment, a considerable period of time may pass before full conservation is realized.

The best adjustment would not force national income down; so borrowing and/or export expansion are the best possibilities. In the short run, the balance-of-payments deficit might be financed by drawing on foreign exchange reserves. Reserves are a form of self-finance, and it gives economic policymakers time to secure other financing. But borrowing only pushes the day of final income reduction into the future unless exports grow by enough in the meantime to offset the deficit and amortize the debt. Thus, although the large oil-induced deficits of the mid-1970s inflicted some damage on all oil-importing countries, these negative effects can be minimized by those countries best able to use reserves, obtain financing, and eventually expand exports.

Balance-of-Payments Adjustment
in Oil-Importing Latin America

We use Latin America to illustrate the diverse ways in which countries have handled the energy crisis. Reserves are the starting point, since they are the means to face the initial, sharp imbalances. External debt positions and export performances indicate how well countries have been able to provide themselves with medium- and long-term solutions. Overall, countries that adjust without suffering sharp reductions in aggregate output weather the crisis adequately.

The Initial Adjustment

Table 7.2 shows the position of each Latin American oil-importing country in early 1974. The thirteen countries examined are divided into three groups, depending upon their ability to manage the very short-run problem. To determine these positions, we calculated net reserves in Column C, and the increase in petroleum import costs between 1973 and 1974 (Column G). We then checked, in Column J, to see whether net reserves would have been adequate to cover the increased expenditures. Group 1 is composed of the five countries that possessed adequate reserves. Countries in Group 2 had reserves that would have been completely used up in financing the increased oil costs, and in the cases of El Salvador and Honduras, additional reserves would have been needed. Group 3 countries all had payments adjustment problems in any event, since in each of these five cases, reserves were inadequate to cover 1974 debt service.

This classification system must be taken as only a rough approximation of degree of difficulty. The increase in petroleum import cost, 1973–1974 (Column G), is simply the difference in the oil-import expenditures in each year. Clearly, some change in petroleum imports would have occurred in any event, since as countries grow, their petroleum imports increase. Thus, Column G overstates the amount of the increased prices. Also, although we have based our classification on net reserves in relation to increased petroleum costs (Column J), we do not imply that using reserves is the way in which extra petroleum expense will actually be covered. Alternatively, export expansion and/or loans could meet the extra expense. But these factors varied from country to country, so we have used Column J to indicate how well countries could have borne the increased energy costs if drawing upon reserves had been the only available means of doing so.

In Group 1, Guatemala held high reserves in relation to its imports (Column E), and petroleum made up only a fairly low proportion of total imports (Columns H and I). The Dominican Republic began 1974 with relatively low reserves, but it was the only country where petroleum imports declined. These two countries were probably in the best position of all oil-importing Latin American countries to withstand the oil price increase. Argentina and Nicaragua began 1974 with relatively low net reserves (Column E), but in both cases, petroleum imports were not large in relation to total imports. Therefore, reserves would have been adequate for adjustment.

Brazil presents a unique problem among Group 1 countries. The country's petroleum imports were 23 percent of total imports in 1974, but since Brazil entered 1974 with immense reserves, adjustment should not have been difficult. Nevertheless, because of its heavy dependence upon imported oil, Brazil was most uncomfortable. Reduction in reserves to more "normal" levels or further oil price rises could (and did) create a difficult situation. Brazil was under the most pressure of all Group 1 countries to obtain longer-run financing, to expand exports, and to cut down on the proportion of petroleum imports.

In Group 2, the oil imports of Honduras and Peru each made up a higher proportion of total imports than the oil imports of any countries in Group 1 except Brazil. In both Honduras and Peru, the increased burden would have reduced net reserves to about zero (had reserves been the sole adjustment mechanism). Some of Peru's problems do not appear on Table 7.2. At the end of 1973, that country's reserves were relatively high, but part of the buildup had come from increased borrowing. Thus, Peru's ability to finance oil cost increases out of reserves depended upon a temporary situation. Reserves would have been expected to fall even without the energy price increase, and the increased debt service would have reduced them even further. There had already been a large jump in Peru's debt service payments between 1972 and 1973.[4] El Salvador and Honduras, meanwhile, held reserves that had not been generated by heavy borrowing. Thus, of the three countries in Group 2, Peru's position was the most precarious.

The five countries in Group 3 had inadequate reserves to meet their

TABLE 7.2
Reserves, Debt Service and Imports, 1974

	International Reserves End 1973	Service on External Debt 1974	Net Reserves (A-B)	Imports 1974	Net Reserve Import Relationship (C/D)%
	A	B	C	D	E
GROUP 1					
Argentina	1149	782	367	3635	10
Brazil	6360	1125	5235	14168	37
Dominican Rep.	84	42	42	819	5
Guatemala	191	27	164	700	23
Nicaragua	116	48	68	560	12
GROUP 2					
El Salvador	41	25	17	564	3
Honduras	42	12	30	391	8
Peru	526	423	103	1018	10
GROUP 3					
Chile	122	278	-156	1911	(-)
Costa Rica	48	51	- 3	666	(-)
Panama	42	135	- 93	822	(-)
Paraguay	57	116	- 59	197	(-)
Uruguay	91	156	- 65	487	(-)

Sources: Service on External Debt is from IDB, External Public Debt of the Latin American Countries; International Economics Section, Washington, D.C., April, 1979; other data from IMF, International Financial Statistics, Washington, D.C., 1979, various pages.

Notes:

Except a, estimates from UN, Economic Commission for Latin America, 1975, pp. 90-91.

Figures in columns A-D, F, G and J are in millions of current dollars.

Table 7.2, cont.

Petroleum Imports 1974	Increase in Petroleum Import Cost 1973-74	Petroleum Imports as % Total Imports 1974	Petroleum Imports as % Total Imports 1973	Net Reserves (1974) minus Increased Petroleum Cost 1973-74 (C-G)
F	G	H	I	J
328	244	9	4	123
3233	2247	23	14	2988
38[a]	-18[a]	5	13[a]	60
80	53	11	6	111
51	34	9	5	34
48	30	9	5	- 13
55	33	14	8	- 3
174[a]	94[a]	17	7[a]	9
412[a]	292[a]	22	8[a]	-448
38	24	6	4	- 27
271	183	33	18	-276
35	29	18	5	- 88
141	96	29	16	-161

justment. Furthermore, with the exception of Costa Rica, these countries had ratios of petroleum imports to total imports that were among the highest in Latin America in 1974. They needed to borrow quickly or to contract economically.

The Longer-Term Adjustment

Table 7.3 evaluates the period since 1974, and the data are for 1977, the last year for which we could obtain comprehensive information on petroleum imports. The net reserve/import relationship in Column E tells us about each country's ability to withstand disturbances to its balance of payments and is comparable to figures for 1973-1974 shown in Table 7.2, Column E. A higher percentage indicates a greater ability.

Eight countries had improved their reserves-to-import relationship, and for those countries for which information was available, all but

TABLE 7.3
Reserves, Debt Service and Imports, 1977

	International Reserves End 1977	Service on External Debt 1977	Net Reserves (A-B)	Imports 1977	Reserve Import Relationship (C/D)%	Petro Imports 1977	Petro Imports as % of Total
	A	B	C	D	E	F	G
GROUP 1							
Argentina	3154	1004	2150	4161	52	338	8
Brazil	7192	3414	3778	13257	28	4201	32
Dominican Rep.	180	64	116	992	12	u	
Guatemala	669	18	651	1083	60	u	
Nicaragua	148	91	57	720	8	78	11
GROUP 2							
El Salvador	211	37	174	947	18	86	9
Honduras	180	41	139	581	24	52	9
Peru	379	652	-273	892	(-)	u	
GROUP 3							
Chile	427	852	-425	2414	(-)	u	
Costa Rica	190	86	104	1021	10	40	4
Panama	71	168	- 97	861	(-)	255	30
Paraguay	268	26	242	302	80	27	9
Uruguay	307	243	64	730	9	186	25

Sources: Same as Table 7.2

u = data unavailable

three had decreased the ratio of oil imports to total imports. Paraguay, Honduras, El Salvador, and Guatemala had been most successful in building reserves despite high petroleum costs. Paraguay had increased its reserves while reducing the proportion of petroleum in total imports from 18 percent to 9 percent. Uruguay also had improved its reserves, but (as we will see below) at some cost. Argentina had greatly increased reserves, thus further improving its initial adequate position. That country also enjoyed a low ratio of petroleum to total imports. Given their initial positions, the Dominican Republic, Costa Rica, and Nicaragua had adequately managed their reserves, though political problems since 1977 have affected Nicaragua's reserve position.

Reserve problems do not appear to have been adequately solved for Chile, Panama, Peru, or Brazil. In 1977, the first two had still been unable to build reserves greater than their debt service. Peru's problem had caused its position to deteriorate considerably. Debt built up before 1973 increasingly interfered with Peru's attempts to adjust its balance of payments. Sharp devaluations of its currency, the sol, have slowed some imports but have not been able to close the trade gap.

Brazil's position deteriorated more than most. Reserves in relation to imports were still high (28 percent) but much below the 1974 level (37 percent). Furthermore, debt service had about tripled. Of all the Latin American countries, only Brazil had experienced a large increase in the ratio of oil imports to total imports (from 23 percent in 1974 to 32 percent in 1977).

To determine whether the reserve positions examined above came only as a result of debt accumulation, we now turn to Table 7.4, which shows the debt service ratios in 1960, 1970, 1973, and 1977. In 1977, some countries were in a stronger debt service position than at the beginning of the seventies, or even a decade before. Argentina, Brazil, Peru, and Chile had been the heaviest borrowers in the region, but later, they were joined by Uruguay and Panama. Except for Brazil, debt service ratios of Group 1 countries were lower, or about the same, in 1977 as they had been in 1973 (or even in 1970). Brazil's problem resulted not only from heavy borrowing, but also from a lag in exports beginning in 1977 (exports expanded by only about 4 percent in 1977–1978). From 1974 to 1976, Brazil's ratio of debt service to exports ranged between 13 and 15.1 percent.

In Group 2, El Salvador's debt service was no greater in 1977 than it had been in 1970. Although debt service had increased somewhat in Honduras by 1977, its ratio to exports remained low. The problem country is Peru, where debt service in 1977 was more than 2.5 times its 1970 level. But, this burden had increased *before* the major oil price hikes, and had remained high throughout the 1973–1977 period.

TABLE 7.4
Debt Service as % of Exports, Various Years

	1960	1970	1973	1977
GROUP 1				
Argentina	20.5	21.7	17.9	15.3
Brazil	38.7	14.3	13.2	25.8
Dominican Rep.	–	6.2	5.7	7.0
Guatemala	1.5	7.4	3.6	1.3
Nicaragua	3.8	10.6	19.1	12.4
GROUP 2				
El Salvador	2.6	3.5	5.3	3.5
Honduras	2.8	3.0	3.7	7.2
Peru	10.5	11.7	29.6	30.5
GROUP 3				
Chile	14.2	19.2	10.9	32.6
Costa Rica	4.8	10.0	10.3	9.0
Panama	1.6	7.6	16.8	19.1
Paraguay	6.8	11.2	10.0	6.4
Uruguay	5.8	21.7	22.9	27.9

Source: Inter-American Development Bank, 1979.

Chile is the problem country in Group 3 since its debt service almost tripled from 1973 to 1977. Panama and Uruguay both carried relatively high debt service in 1977, but in each case, the increase since 1973 had been moderate, and for Uruguay, a high burden can be traced back at least to 1970.

The region's poorest performers in economic growth from 1973 to 1977 were Argentina, Chile, Peru, and Panama. The data in Table 7.5 show growth in GDP and exports, adjusted for price changes, and in each of those four countries, the economy was stagnant. In the rest of the region, however, countries continued to have rates that were either above their average for the preceding decade (four cases) or else had declined but were nevertheless historically high for LDCs. Except for the four countries mentioned, the region grew at an (unweighted) average rate of 5.4 percent.

Despite petroleum price increases, sustained growth occurred through the 1970s. Massad (1978) observed that as a group, non-petroleum-exporting Latin American countries grew faster than the OECD

TABLE 7.5
Real Rates of Growth: GDP and Exports

	GDP		Exports	
	1973-74	1974-77	1973-74	1974-77
GROUP 1				
Argentina	4.1	-0.2	9.1	5.9
Brazil	7.7	6.4	17.1	7.9
Dominican Rep.	6.3	5.3	33.1	-0.1
Guatemala	5.7	5.9	20.1	19.9
Nicaragua	4.8	5.4	26.1	11.9
GROUP 2				
El Salvador	5.2	4.9	18.1	22.9
Honduras	5.0	4.3	2.1	12.9
Peru	5.1	1.7	0.1	-13.2
GROUP 3				
Chile	3.2	0.0	90.1	-11.1
Costa Rica	7.1	5.5	7.1	19.9
Panama	7.4	0.4	42.1	- 1.1
Paraguay	4.8	8.1	23.1	10.9
Uruguay	1.1	3.3	8.1	9.9

Source: IMF, International Financial Statistics, September
1979.

(industrialized) countries. For this reason, it is very difficult to assess the impact of increased prices on LDCs. The business cycle in LDCs follows that in MDCs (see for example Hargreaves-Heap 1979). The worldwide recession of 1974–1975 was expected to depress incomes in LDCs, since demand for the latter's exports depend upon income levels in MDCs. To grow while MDCs contract, LDCs would need both capital and an expansion of exports. Even without petroleum price increases, we should have expected income and export growth rates to dip in 1974–1975.

Table 7.5 shows that although export growth dropped from 1974 to 1977, in most cases it went from very high to moderate levels. Immediately before 1974, exports of most Latin American countries were growing rapidly, so all countries experienced a drop in exports in 1974–1977, compared to 1973–1974, except some Central American countries and Uruguay. Despite declines in export growth rates, Paraguay, Nicaragua, and Brazil continued to turn in a strong export performance. Only in the Dominican Republic, Panama, Chile, and Peru were exports sharply curtailed from 1974 to 1977. In the latter two countries, the decline was distorted by record copper prices in 1974. Those high prices came after lows in 1973; therefore, they artificially raised 1974 exports as a point of reference.

Argentina's declining growth rate to approximately zero from 1974 to 1977 would normally have made adjustment difficult, but Argentina is an oil producer, and its petroleum imports are a relatively small part of its total imports. Argentina also successfully reduced that proportion even further between 1974 and 1977. In addition, its rate of export expansion (5.9 percent) has been adequate to prevent the balance of payments from deteriorating and to reduce the debt service burden.

Uruguay is in a sensitive position as it has a high dependency on oil (25 percent of imports in 1977). Nevertheless, that fact does not seem to have been overly burdensome; the growth rates in GDP and in exports both increased from 1974 to 1977, and its negative reserves of 1974 had become positive by 1977, despite the oil price increases. This improvement stemmed from vigorous export growth, combined with an ability to borrow. Despite heavy borrowing, Uruguay's debt service burden increased only slightly over the traditionally high level.

In summary, most oil-importing Latin American economies have performed well, given the balance-of-payments strain of increased oil prices and recession in the more-developed world. For the most part, sustained growth has accompanied expanding exports, without extraordinary debt accumulation.[5] ECLA (UN, ECLA 1979) indicates that exports and imports of non-oil-exporting Latin American countries[6] have increased at about the same rate (exports, 20.9 percent; imports, 20.2 percent, unweighted yearly averages) since 1972, despite the large import jump in 1974 due to oil price increases. Since 1975, exports have expanded by 12.8 percent per year, and imports by only 5.3 percent.

The Poor Performers in Latin America

Unfortunately, a few countries have not fared well. Peru, Chile, and Panama have performed poorly on reserve management, growth, and export performance, and Brazil has shown some signs of a weakening position. These countries merit closer attention.

Chile and Peru

The problems of Chile and Peru predate the energy crisis. At the end of 1973, Chile was basically bankrupt. Public debt service could not be maintained, and a major rescheduling was required. Inflation was running at over 300 percent per year, despite the GDP reductions in

1972 and 1973.[7] The large borrowings and recessionary conditions that characterized almost the entire 1974-1977 period were associated with the public austerity program. These conditions probably would have occurred in any event, no matter what had happened to petroleum prices.

Peru's difficulties were also evident before the oil price increases in late 1973. Large public investment programs began about 1970. Unfortunately, tax revenues lagged far behind expenditures, and public enterprises produced financial losses rather than the profits that had been projected. Thus, by 1972, Peru was forced to borrow heavily, and it turned to private foreign banks. These banks responded willingly, in part because oil had been discovered in Peru in 1971, and a "new Saudi Arabia" was envisaged. Peru "mortgaged" petroleum reserves that did not materialize. By 1974, the current-account deficit was about 40 percent of exports, but this deficit was masked by capital inflows large enough to turn an overall surplus (on an official settlements basis). The current-account deficit was compounded by poor export performance and a greatly overvalued exchange rate.[8] By 1975, the country was badly overextended, and several abrupt stabilization programs were enacted during 1976 and 1977. By 1978, Peru was being kept from bankruptcy by forty-five to ninety-day debt "rollovers" by private banks. Restrictions had become severe, and civil disruptions have occurred since that time.

Brazil

Brazil's attempts to grow at "miracle" rates of 10-11 percent proved sustainable only because of infusions of new capital. But heavy borrowing depends on a rapid expansion of exports and imports being held in check. By 1972-1973, Brazil had a balance-of-payments surplus (on an official settlements basis), despite a current-account deficit, because of large inflows of foreign capital. Because of new borrowing, reserves climbed steadily and acted as a "backup" for still new loans (Smith 1979, pp. 305-306). The potential increase in the money supply due to new reserves was only partially offset by monetary policy during 1973. By 1974, the expanding money supply led to excess demand, which in turn caused a surge of imports and a deterioration in the balance of payments. Although oil imports increased by $2,247 million between 1973 and 1974, largely due to the oil price increases, total imports expanded by $7,169 million. Thus, petroleum price hikes compounded Brazil's balance-of-payments problem, but they were by no means decisive. In Smith's words, "The importance of petroleum in Brazil's current predicament is easily exaggerated" (1979, p. 306).

Panama

Panama is one of the most oil-dependent countries in Latin America. As a proportion of total imports, oil ranged between 33 percent in 1974 and 30 percent in 1977. There was some borrowing to cover this deficit, but it was not heavy. Debt service increased slightly between 1973 and 1977.[9] Exports have not grown, and in real purchasing power, they declined slightly from 1973 to 1977. Since the increased balance-of-payments deficit was neither financed in the short run nor closed by increased exports in the longer run, Panama's annual growth rate predictably dropped from the very high levels preceding 1973 (7.4 percent) to only 0.4 percent from 1974 to 1977.

Oil Prices and Economic Growth

General statements about the impact of increased petroleum import costs upon economic growth are still speculative. We do not know what would have been done with the increased amounts that were spent on petroleum imports had petroleum prices not risen. Nor do we know how petroleum imports would have risen in any event in response to the rapid growth occurring in some Latin American countries.

In Table 7.6, we have calculated the annual increase in petroleum import cost (1973–1977) as a percentage of 1977 gross domestic investment (GDI) for each Latin American country. In only five countries did the increase amount to more than 10 percent of GDI. In Chile and Uruguay, increased petroleum import costs were equivalent to about 25 percent of GDI, but both countries had the lowest investment rates in Latin America. Had they both shown rates of GDI in proportion to GDP equivalent to the average of the other countries shown (22 percent of GDP), increased petroleum import costs would have been only 10.7 percent of GDI in Chile and 15.4 percent of GDI in Uruguay. Panama stands out as paying a very high price, in relation to GDI, for increased petroleum imports.

An extreme estimate of the negative growth impact of increased imported petroleum expenditures on GDP growth rates could be made by assuming that the entire increase could have been invested. Surely, it would not have been, so such an estimate as the one shown in the last column of Table 7.6 must be considered a maximum negative growth effect. In making this calculation, we have assumed an incremental capital-output ratio (ICOR) of 3, which is on the low side, since most empirical estimates of ICOR fall above 3. Also, excess capacity existed in some of these countries, so the ICOR for them would have been considerably above 3. Even with these extreme assumptions, the negative growth

TABLE 7.6
Oil Import Costs and Investment

141

	Increase in Annual Petroleum Import Costs (Million $) 1973-77	Gross Domestic Investment as % GDP 1977	Gross Domestic Investment (Million $) 1977	Increase in Annual Petroleum Costs as % 1977 GDI	Maximum Negative Impact on GDP Growth Rate
GROUP 1					
Argentina	254	19	8,456	3.0	0.2
Brazil	3,215	22	34,737	9.2	0.7
Dominican Rep.	-18	25	1,050	-1.7	positive
Guatemala	53	20	1,011	5.2	.3
Nicaragua	61	25	498	12.2	1.0
GROUP 2					
El Salvador	68	22	508	13.4	1.0
Honduras	30	24	325	9.2	0.7
Peru	94*	15	2,066	4.5	0.2
GROUP 3					
Chile	292*	9	1,107	26.4	0.8
Costa Rica	26	23	599	4.3	0.3
Panama	167	22	483	34.6	2.5
Paraguay	21	25	511	4.1	0.3
Uruguay	141	14	581	24.3	1.1

Sources: UN, Economic Commission for Latin America, 1975, pp. 90-91; IDB, External Public Debt of the Latin American Countries, International Economics Section, Washington, D.C., April 1979; and World Bank, World Development Report, 1979, New York: Oxford University Press, 1979, various pages.

*The increase shown in 1973-74. 1977 data were not available at the time of writing.

impact is not large in most cases. Panama has probably been most adversely affected. The other "problem" countries—Argentina, Chile, and Peru—would still be growing slowly even if their growth rates were augmented by the rates shown in the last column of Table 7.6. The figures in that column would be reduced by about two-thirds if we had assumed that only one-half of the increased amount spent on petroleum imports had been invested and an ICOR of 4 had been projected.

Conclusion

Oil price increases have adversely affected non-oil-exporting less developed countries, and it could be expected that they would suffer similar effects if general price increases of primary products were enforced through NIEO. But LDCs are resilient. Even under the adverse conditions caused by both oil price increases and stagnant MDC economies, the Latin American countries have been able to expand both their incomes and their exports—except for some countries whose difficulties stem from other sources.

We have surveyed the balance-of-payments adjustment problems of oil-importing Latin American countries for the period of the so-called energy crisis. For the most part, those countries did not suffer an economic contraction, and when they did, the difficulties are traceable to non-energy-related factors. Even countries that could not have been considered in sound economic health in 1974 (i.e., those in Group 3) were able to improve their positions greatly. Costa Rica, Paraguay, and Uruguay each ended 1977 in much better shape than they ended 1973, although Uruguay may have overly relied upon a "Brazilian" model and may expect "Brazilian" problems in the future.

Among the problem countries, the political turmoils in Chile and Argentina would make economic progress unlikely no matter what happened to petroleum prices. Peru has been beset by economic mismanagement, political difficulties, and bad luck—all of which began before 1973. Brazil faces a petroleum problem, but that problem has not affected the country as much as adverse adjustments to its own economic growth strategy begun before 1973. These conclusions deal only with rough orders of magnitude, since compounding factors, such as recession in the OECD countries, cannot be adequately accounted for. Nevertheless, even extreme assumptions do not show that the energy crisis was a primary force affecting Latin American development one way or another in the 1970s.

The lesson from the Latin American example is that the oil price increases of the 1970s were not necessarily disastrous for economic growth. Borrowing and reserve management can be used as short-run measures for balance-of-payments adjustment. Export expansion is the key to long-run adjustment and sustained growth.

Notes

1. Portions of this section were previously published in John P. Powelson, "The Oil Price Increase: Impacts on Industrialized and Less Developed Countries," *Journal of Energy and Development* 3:1 (Autumn 1977), 10–25, and in John P. Powelson, "Oil Prices and the World Balance of Payments," in Ragaei El Mallakh, ed., *OPEC: Twenty Years and Beyond* (Boulder, Colo.: Westview Press, 1981), pp. 175–192.

2. The difference in starting years was caused by slightly different categories in the presentations by the International Monetary Fund, which made it impossible to yield consistent combinations if the same starting year were used. In either case, only rough-order magnitudes are claimed, and inconsistencies are believed minor.

3. This section is adapted from William Loehr, "Post-1973 Adjustment Problems of Oil-Importing Latin American Countries," in H. Munoz, ed., *Desarrollo energético en América Latina y la economía mundial* (Santiago: Editorial Universitaria, 1980).

4. Peru's debt service rose from 15.8 percent of exports in 1972 to 29.6 percent in 1973.

5. For more on the assessment of the debt situation, see Smith 1979.

6. ECLA's definition of non-oil-exporting countries includes countries in addition to those examined here.

7. Ironically, Chile may have been helped by the OPEC activities of late 1973. Many raw materials purchasers anticipated that "other OPECs" would be formed among raw materials exporting countries. Thus, in the rush to stockpile before prices rose, raw materials prices were bid up to record high levels. Copper prices rose so much that Chile's merchandise balance was *positive* in 1974, despite oil increases (Boletín, Banco Central de Chile, Santiago, 1979).

8. As a percentage of GDP, exports in 1974 were only 50 percent of 1964 levels. The sol was pegged at 38.7 = $1 through 1974. Thereafter it devalued rapidly to 196 = $1 by 1978, and 609 = $1 by April 1982.

9. From about 17 percent of exports in 1973 to 19 percent in 1977.

Bibliography

Bird, G. "The Choice Between Balance of Payments Adjustment and Financing." *Malayan Economic Review* 23:2 (October 1978), 16–20.

Cohen, S. D. "Changes in the International Economy: Old Realities and New Myths." *Journal of World Trade Law* 12:4 (July–August 1978), 273–287.

Hargreaves-Heap, S. P. "The Post-War International Business Cycle." *Journal of Economic Studies* 6:1 (May 1979).

Inter-American Development Bank. *External Public Debt of the Latin American Countries.* Economic and Social Development Department, International Economics Section. Washington, D.C., 1979.

International Monetary Fund (IMF), *International Financial Statistics.* Washington, D.C., September 1979.

Loehr, William. "Post-1973 Adjustment Problems of Oil-Importing Latin American Countries." in *Desarrollo energético en América Latina y la economía mundial,* edited by H. Munoz, pp. 214–240. Santiago: Editorial Universitaria, 1980.

Massad, C. "Cartera de inversiones de los países exportadores de petróleo: Diversificación orientada hacia América Latina." *Estudios de economía,* no. 12 (Second semester 1978), 147–172.

Organization for Economic Cooperation and Development (OECD). *Development Cooperation: 1980 Review.* Paris, 1980.

Powelson, John P. "The Oil Price Increase: Impacts on Industrialized and Less Developed Countries." *Journal of Energy and Development* 3:1 (Autumn 1977), 10–25.

————. "Oil Prices and the World Balance of Payments." In *OPEC: Twenty Years and Beyond,* edited by Ragaei El Mallakh, pp. 175–192. Boulder, Colo.: Westview Press, 1981.

Smith, G. W. "The External Debt Prospects of the Non-Oil-Exporting Developing Countries." In *Policy Alternatives for a New International Economic Order,* edited by W. R. Cline, pp. 287–329. New York: Praeger, 1979.

United Nations, Economic Commission for Latin America (ECLA). *América Latina y los problemas actuales de la energía.* Mexico City: Fondo de Cultura Económica, 1975.

————. "La evolución económica de América Latina en 1978." Mimeograph. Santiago, 1979.

8

Other Provisions

The major thrusts of the NIEO plan have now been covered. As we turn to the "minor thrusts," the decision on where to stop is arbitrary. The eighty-five subdivisions in the UN declaration cover virtually all the problems of economic development. We have selected three of them for discussion here: food production, foreign aid, and foreign investment. Another topic of importance—the LDC share of world manufacturing exports—is set forth in the declaration, but we have treated it along with the Generalized System of Preferences (Chapter 3).

Food Production

In recent decades, increases in agricultural output in the third world have kept slightly ahead of population growth, but in some countries, they have run behind. Even the slight increases are usually absorbed by people with rising incomes, who improve their consumption, so that the diet of the poor remains grossly inadequate. In much of the third world, the threats of drought and famine are ever present, just as they were in Europe before the nineteenth century.

Among other propositions, the NIEO plan (I, 2, f and g) calls for efforts "to ensure that developing countries can import the necessary quantity of food without undue strain on their foreign exchange resources ... [and] to ensure that concrete measures to increase food production and storage facilities in developing countries should be introduced."

There is no doubt that food is *the* major problem of the poor. The Food and Agriculture Organization has estimated (1975, p. 22) that sixty-one out of ninety-seven LDCs had a deficit of food in 1970 and that in the Far East and Africa, 25 percent and 30 percent, respectively, of the population suffer from significant malnutrition. In an earlier work (Loehr and Powelson 1981, pp. 79-94), we have assembled other data of a similar, disquieting nature.

In that same book (pp. 223-242), we cite a number of studies that show that programs in nutrition, health, and education would have a high economic payoff, in that over their lifetimes, people who are well nourished, in good health, and well educated will produce material values far in excess of the discounted costs necessary to bring them up to high standards of nutrition, health, and education in the first place. All of those benefits would be in addition to the satisfaction of being well fed, healthy, and educated. But time and again, such programs are simply not undertaken by governments.

Why not? Some critics have tried to put the blame on multinational corporations (Lappé and Collins 1977) for interfering with food production or for converting prime land to export products. But we consider this reasoning to be part of the persistent tendency on the part of well-meaning individuals in MDCs to shift the blame for underdevelopment to themselves or to their fellow countrymen.

To us, the reason is more simple. Although nutrition, health, and education have high payoffs, these payoffs occur in the distant future, and the time horizon for politicians is short. Also, their budgets respond to crises and momentary pressures, and hunger is not momentary and exciting. It is long-term, endemic, and debilitating, and the people who suffer from it do not have high political leverage. Therefore, programs to overcome hunger have been low on the scale of LDC politicians.

How should the well-fed, industrialized world respond? The question is not one of economics, and economists have no expertise that others may not possess. But our common sense leads us to the following twofold response.

First, the world community should be sensitive to starving people. A world emergency food reserve should be established to meet periodic famines as they occur anywhere. (Such a reserve is not specifically mentioned in NIEO.)

Second, the longer-run solution to food problems must lie within the LDCs themselves. With proper policies, almost all LDCs are capable of increasing their food output sufficiently to feed their people—even if all land suited to export crops is used to raise those crops. In most countries, there is enough other land to produce adequately for local consumption if modern agricultural techniques are taught, if storage facilities are supplied, if credit is extended to small farmers, and if farm-to-market roads are built. For the few countries that cannot produce enough food, the answer is to increase other exports so the food can be imported. But we see nothing proper about an international order in which LDCs would *rely* on imports as a major source of food.

What, then, is left for an international order? Not very much. The international community should be sensitive to malnutrition and starvation; it should be prepared to supply experts (but beware—agriculture is highly location-specific, and local farmers may understand more than the foreign experts do); and it should offer loans that are appropriate for rural development.

Except for a world food stabilization fund, these guidelines appear to us to be all the industrialized world can or should offer. We also sense that assigning food a place in an international order is somehow symptomatic of the tendency of LDC governments to place into international orbit those domestic problems that they have themselves persistently and systematically refused to address.

We fear that if MDCs supply food regularly (as through U.S. Food for Peace), such programs will become a substitute for local production, will discourage domestic farmers (who have frequently complained of this foreign competition), and will diminish the necessity for local governments to take the actions that are necessary to increase farm output. The ability to import food always reduces the political leverage of domestic farmers.

Foreign Aid

The NIEO plan calls for more foreign aid, referred to euphemistically as "foreign resource transfer" (II, 2, a). In debates in UNCTAD, third world leaders have long asked for foreign aid of 1 percent—more recently, 0.7 percent—of the gross national products (GNPs) of MDCs. In the decade 1969-1979, official assistance from Development Assistance Committee (DAC) countries (which include MDCs in Europe, North America, Oceania, and Japan) amounted to about 0.4 percent of their GNPs. The U.S. proportion has been in the neighborhood of 0.3 percent, though it fell to 0.24 percent in 1979 (OECD 1980, pp. 180-181).

We are of two minds on foreign aid. The first is that aid should be supplied to the poor so they can increase their productive capabilities. Not only that, but we would put no limit on the amount of aid; it could be several percentage points of the GNPs of MDCs. The second is that an international order consisting of perpetual subsidies of poor countries by rich ones does not provide a dignified life for the recipients. We compromise by suggesting that although foreign aid itself may be indefinite, any category of people (such as particular countries) should receive it only temporarily. Indeed, this procedure has been followed for several countries (including, for example, Mexico and Taiwan).

In 1973, the Congress of the United States mandated "new directions" in foreign aid: Aid should be aimed at the basic needs of the world's poorest. The World Bank also declared that the bulk of its aid would be channeled into rural development (although more recently, energy has also commanded priority).

Whether the mandates of the United States or the World Bank have indeed been met is a matter of much debate. In aggregate terms, U.S. aid is clearly being directed toward social programs. In the 1981 budget authorization request, $1.5 billion was allocated to agriculture, rural development, nutrition, population planning, health, education, and development of the Sahel (plus minor "selected development activities"), and $0.3 billion was allocated to international agencies (U.S., AID 1980, p. 26). But a large part of the aid program ($2.0 billion) was devoted to "security supporting assistance," or compensatory aid to countries devoting part of their own economic resources to defense deemed to be in the interest of the United States.

Whether aid is actually reaching the poor depends on an analysis of individual projects. There are indeed many projects in rural areas— including farm-to-market roads, technical assistance for agriculture, and the like. One critic, Roy Prosterman of the University of Washington Law School, graded a number of projects for their efficiency in directing benefits to the poor at reasonable cost (Crittenden 1978) and found wide variations. Two recent studies of the World Bank show diverse evaluations: Hürni (1980) gives the Bank high marks, but van de Laar (1980), a former Bank staff member, criticizes it for not really reaching the poor.

We cannot evaluate this debate in a short space. Rather, we express other doubts about the role of financial assistance in a world economic order. We favor direct aid to the poor for immediate and humanitarian motives. But in development, which alone will sustain the long-tun standards of living of the poor, the LDCs must partially shift away from primary production and into manufacturing. Foreign aid may be expected (in small quantities) for rural development and small-scale agriculture, because those activities do not threaten the economic interests of the donor countries, but foreign aid has not been given to promote manufacturing, nor is it likely to be in the future.

The LDCs must face squarely their conflict of interest with MDCs. Development means coming into competition with the MDCs (as Japan has done), and the MDCs are *not* going to help the LDCs do that (a point the Japanese well understood). It is no coincidence that the NICs have turned progressively away from using foreign aid. Some people would argue that the NICs did so because their success removed the need for aid; others (like us) would say that removal of the need helps explain the NICs' success.

Finally, we note the advice of P. T. Bauer:

> Relief of poverty is a much canvassed objective of aid, and one with moral overtones. But *official* aid does not go to poor people. . . . It goes

to their rulers whose spending policies are determined by their own personal and political interests, among which the position of the poorest has very low priority. [Bauer 1980, p. 24]

Foreign Investment

The NIEO plan also calls for "promotion of foreign investment both public and private from developed to developing countries in accordance with the needs and requirements of their economies as determined by the recipient countries" (II, 2, c).

How much foreign investment now flows from MDCs to LDCs? How does this foreign capital compare with investment from domestic sources? Because the data for many countries are sketchy, these questions are not easy to answer in the aggregate. The World Bank cautiously does not give totals in its *World Tables* or in its annual *World Development Report*. If we are content with wide-order magnitudes, however, we can make some approximations.[1] Using World Bank data, we estimate that in 1978, domestic investment for ninety low- and middle-income LDCs was approximately $327 billion. They received (net of repayments) about $51 billion of foreign capital (not including bank loans), of which $44 billion was from public funds, and $7 billion from private direct investment (such as from MNCs). Thus, LDCs financed approximately 84 percent of their own investment and relied on foreign capital for 16 percent (of which 2 percent was private, and almost 14 percent public). These data confirm our conclusions in Chapter 4—that multinational corporations supply only a small percentage of LDC investment.

But how can this situation be? Are these not poor countries caught in the vicious cycle of poverty with little left over to save?

First, domestic investment includes not only investment by large companies and government, but also the thousands of small shops and artisan factories throughout each country.

Second, although the absolute poor cannot save (for they are on the margin of starvation), there are still many middle poor who can. In an earlier study of a rural community in Kenya (Loehr and Powelson 1979), we observed that perceived investment opportunities (such as in a small shop requiring very little capital) are the principal incentive for rural people to save.

We believe that those are the kinds of saving and investment that need to be encouraged in LDCs. Village artisanry, as well as small factories in the urban bazaar (or informal economy), employ large numbers of people in labor-intensive industries, but they are not the kinds of investment made by foreign capital.

But should not foreign capital be encouraged anyway? Perhaps so, but we are lukewarm about the idea. When the same people who criticize MNCs for their alleged distortions also urge greater flows of foreign investment, we see some inconsistency. In Chapter 4, we criticized LDC governments for providing too much domestic credit (through low interest rates) to foreign and other capital-intensive industries. This is capital that might alternatively be made available to the enterprises of the poor—through credits to small-scale farmers and village artisans.

It is hard to know where to strike the balance. At worst, additional foreign investment may harm the poor by sifting off complementary domestic capital, and at best, it might do them some minimal good by providing employment and teaching new skills. There are no data that can help us reach a definitive opinion.

Our tentative opinion, however, is that no more concessional funds are warranted. These funds might well end up lining the pockets of the rich, and we see no reasonable way in which they would materially trickle down to the poor. We believe that the rich should pay market rates for the funds they borrow internationally and that the world market is available to them if they have sound projects (and, unfortunately, even sometimes when they do not).

Conclusion

In this chapter, we have briefly treated three points of NIEO: food, foreign aid, and foreign investment. Although a world food policy is badly needed (particularly for emergencies), we see no need for major revisions in the world structures that handle foreign aid or foreign investment. Nothing in these areas would call for a new "order" in international economic relations.

All the points we have made about NIEO, in the present and preceding chapters, are closely related to the domestic policies of the LDC governments in ways that we believe have not always been clear to NIEO supporters. We turn to these domestic policies in the next chapter.

Notes

1. From the World Bank's *World Development Report, 1980*: By multiplying per capita GNP by population (p. 110), we estimate total GNP for ninety low- and middle-income LDCs. By applying average percentages for gross domestic investment (p. 118), we estimate the domestic investment for these same countries. Because data for a small number of countries are missing, the Bank does not

add up the flows of external capital (public and private) on pages 136–137. Our guess is that flows from the missing countries are small or negligible, and therefore we did add up those for the remaining countries. The results are what we label wide-order magnitudes. Not included is portfolio capital (e.g., bank loans).

Bibliography

Bauer, P. T. "The Harm That Foreign Aid Does." *Wall Street Journal,* June 9, 1980.

Crittenden, Ann. "A Tough Report Card for A.I.D. Program." *New York Times,* February 26, 1978.

Food and Agriculture Organization. *Food and Nutrition* (Rome) 1:1 (1975).

Hürni, Bettina S. *The Lending Policy of the World Bank in the 1970s.* Boulder, Colo.: Westview Press, 1980.

Lappé, Frances Moore, and Collins, Joseph. *Food First: Beyond the Myth of Scarcity.* Boston: Houghton Mifflin, 1977.

Loehr, William, and Powelson, John P. "An Accounting Analysis of Rural Business in Kenya." UNIDO, *Industry and Development* (Vienna) 4:30–50 (1979).

————. *The Economics of Development and Distribution.* New York: Harcourt, Brace, Jovanovich, 1981.

Organization for Economic Cooperation and Development (OECD). *Development Cooperation: 1980 Review.* Paris, 1980.

United States, Agency for International Development (AID). *Congressional Report for Fiscal Year 1980: Main Volume.* Washington, D.C., 1980.

van de Laar, Aart. *The World Bank and the Poor.* Boston: Martinus Nijhoff, 1980.

World Bank. *World Development Report, 1980.* New York: Oxford University Press for the World Bank, 1980.

9

The Internal Gap

Advocates of NIEO are aware that an internal gap divides the people of LDCs into rich and poor. In general, they have thought of the internal gap as similar to, even paralleling, the international gap. Often they presume, therefore, that the internal gap must be treated in the same way as the international gap: better terms of trade for farmers (vis-à-vis manufacturers), more rural credit, rural participation in national planning, and the like.

We agree with all these points, but they do not constitute the major problem. The internal and international gaps are not parallel, but the lines cross, and where they cross, we find the principal forces underlying the internal gap. It is the internal gap that LDCs must close for development to proceed.

The internal gap—known to economists as dualism—has two main dimensions. Economic dualism refers to a wide dispersion of wealth: a few very wealthy people living close to many on the verge of starvation. Technological dualism is found when the most modern and the most primitive methods of production exist side by side. It occurs in agriculture when large farms employ the latest machinery, and small farms rely on ox-drawn wooden plows. It occurs in industry when artisans work with hand tools only blocks away from large-scale, automated factories.

How Are the Gaps Sustained?

Economists spend a lot of time discussing the origins of the gaps: whether they occurred in tribal and in preindustrial societies; whether they inevitably widen with economic growth or only sometimes. We have ourselves indulged at some length in this debate (Loehr and Powelson 1981), and we do not wish to repeat ourselves here. The important reality is that the gaps are there. Our conclusion is that whether or not the gaps normally widen with economic growth, they need not do so.

153

We digress to put an oft-debated point to rest. Whether or not the gaps widen does not depend on whether a country is socialist or capitalist. The gaps have narrowed in socialist and capitalist societies alike: in Japan, North and South Korea, both Chinas (People's Republic and Taiwan), Hong Kong, and Singapore. They have remained wide in countries that call themselves socialist, such as Tanzania and Ethiopia; countries that call themselves mixtures, such as Zambia, Mexico, and Peru under Juan Velasco Alvarado; and countries that are clearly capitalist, such as Kenya, Nigeria, and Brazil.

There is a set of government policies that seems to be associated with sustaining the gaps, whatever the nature of the government. Whether these policies are a "conspiracy" on the part of the rich may be debated, but we do not think so. Instead, we believe that governments "fall into" the policies with all good intentions. Two misconceptions are responsible: first, that a lack of capital is the prime reason for underdevelopment and second, that both the internal affairs and the foreign policies of LDCs must be managed by the rich and the educated for the benefit of the poor. It is in connection with these misconceptions that the internal gaps and the NIEO intersect.

Three areas of policymaking are affected: the contribution of agriculture, direct intervention by government, and indirect intervention.

The Contribution of Agriculture

The belief that capital is the missing ingredient in economic development led to the question of where to find it. Foreign sources would not be enough, and since LDCs are primarily agrarian, agriculture must supply the capital. Farmers' savings would supply capital for urban industry, and migration from countryside to city would provide the labor (Lewis 1955). Economic history has been interpreted to support this belief. Agricultural revolutions have always preceded industrial revolutions, and farmers in England provided the capital for the early shops and factories.

But two historical points have been downplayed. One is that agriculture improved *first*, which enabled farmers to save part of their higher incomes. The other point is that in England and Europe, the farmers saved voluntarily, and they themselves decided when and where to invest in industry. As a result, much industry was rural and originally associated with farming activities. Furthermore, along with the flow of capital to urban areas, there were also reverse flows as many industrialists found the countryside more attractive than the city.

In today's LDCs, by contrast, government elites have paid little attention to *developing* agriculture and more to *squeezing* it. Their disdain for the poor has led them to believe that the farmers would not invest in industry if let alone; therefore, government agencies must extract the investment. In many LDCs, farmers are required by law to sell major crops only to government marketing boards. The excuse has been that these boards would store crops between harvests to assure an even flow throughout the year, and thereby damp down the price cycles. It is, of course, believed that "ignorant" farmers are not capable of storing their crops themselves.

Naturally, the marketing boards must pay their operating expenses, and their directors must be paid salaries (and perquisites) commensurate with their dignity. Consequently, the terms of trade are turned against farmers in many countries, not by the normal forces of supply and demand, but by deliberate government action. The profits of marketing boards presumably are turned over to the government for investment in "development projects" (Bauer 1972, pp. 369–386), but they may also be sometimes used for political payoffs.

In addition to the marketing boards, the agricultural squeeze has been undertaken through price controls. Farm prices are to be kept low in the interests of the urban workers, who are essential to the modern factories. In many countries (such as Argentina under Perón), the farms became decapitalized so that agricultural improvements were impossible.

These policies have been a principal force behind the neglect of agriculture in LDCs and a main reason why food output is scarcely keeping up with population growth. A few economists, such as Owen (1966), were able to predict the results; but not many were so prescient.

But, is not the internal gap similar to the international one? Just as we are now suggesting better terms of trade for farmers in LDCs, does not NIEO call for better terms for primary producers? Superficially, the gaps appear the same. But the similarity soon ends. Internationally, there are no government controls on primary-product prices.[1] For the most part, primary products are admitted free of duty into MDCs (in the United States, virtually all primary products enter free), because they are needed for industry. NIEO calls for an imposition of controls to restrict output and raise primary-product prices above the market. Internally, by contrast, controls already exist in most LDCs, and they depress prices *below* the market. A return to market pricing, and a release of farmers from obligations to sell to government agencies, would raise prices for farmers and give them incentive to increase output, which would possibly supply the necessary margin for investment in improved techniques or even to start artisan industries on the farms.

In short, LDC government elites are trying to play both ends into the middle, and they themselves are in the middle. Through NIEO, they want to channel international resources to themselves. Since most export commodities must be sold through a government or its agencies, the elites need not pass the benefits on to farmers or the poorer workers. By controlling prices and the channels available to the farmers, they direct any surplus to themselves. It is here that the NIEO plan intersects, rather than parallels, internal-gap policy.

Direct Intervention and the Barton Gap

What do governments do with the surpluses they have taxed or obtained through price and sales restrictions? Elsewhere we have likened the governments of LDCs today to the benevolent despots of Europe in the eighteenth century (Loehr and Powelson 1981, pp. 28–30). Both these elites believed that only they were able to direct the affairs of the poor, to the benefit of the latter. Since the poor are "not capable" of starting their own businesses, the government must do it for them.

This belief stands in the way of burgeoning industry that is undertaken by the poor. In every large city in the LDCs, textile production, artisanry, tailoring, clothing shops, bicycle repair work, and above all, retailing have been started by the poor. This activity completely belies the theory that the poor are unable to save, or that they have no business sense. Yet for the most part, government planners not only ignore the bazaar economy, they actively discourage it. Most countries provide little or no infrastructure (paved roads, schools, electricity, transport, garbage collection) in areas occupied by the bazaar economy. Many consider it an urban blight, and they push it to the outskirts, out of the sight of tourists.

Instead, many LDC governments provide infrastructure, loans, and even physical facilities to modern industries. They also set up government enterprises, known in some countries (e.g., Tanzania and Zambia) as parastatal companies, which often are autonomous and unaudited; they presumably report to some ministry but in fact report to no one. They may earn profits because they are monopolies, and no one checks on their inefficiencies. The salaries of the top officials of parastatal companies are reputed to be much higher than those of their counterparts elsewhere. In some countries, parastatal companies have the sole right to engage in certain industries, whether they actually do so or not. This dog-in-the-manger approach keeps smaller enterprises out. Private persons are not allowed to produce in the reserved areas, yet the needed goods and services may not be produced at all.

Local harassment adds to the burden of the small, private producer. In a study of the Republic of South Vietnam, Barton (1974) reasoned that small-scale producers fear their own growth, for once they reach a certain size, they become subject to demands (payoffs for licenses, permissions) from petty, local bureaucrats. In smallness, they find obscurity. Therefore, when they do accumulate capital, they tend to invest in other small enterprises rather than to expand the original one. Hence, they cannot enjoy economies of scale. Very large enterprises (say, over 100 employees), on the other hand, learn to cope with the petty bureaucrats; hence, they can survive. Barton was trying to explain why he saw few middle-sized enterprises, of about 25 to 50 employees. We refer to their absence as the "Barton gap."

All capital devoted to parastatal enterprises, or to other costly government projects, is capital that might have been used to aid the poor, such as through agricultural credit or the development of rural industries.

In many ways, NIEO is designed to place still more capital into the hands of the government elites. We have already shown that debt forgiveness would principally benefit the rich, just as higher prices for primary products would. Likewise, more foreign aid, more investment into LCD economic sectors as determined by the recipient countries, and SDRs allocated to LDC governments would add to the resources of people who are already rich. Alternatively, these funds might also increase the productivity of the poor.

Indirect Intervention

Indirect government intervention occurs when policies such as taxation and interest rates change incentives, so that individuals and businesses behave differently from the way they would have behaved if left alone.

In keeping with the philosophy that governments must manage development, LDC policymakers in the early fifties wanted to produce more items locally. What more appropriate place to look for possible new items than in the list of imports? There were products for which demand had been proved, and local producers could replace foreign suppliers. The process became known as import substitution industrialization (ISI). Latin American countries were the pioneers in ISI; Asian and African countries soon followed.

With some variations according to countries, the ISI "policy package" consists of the following factors.

Low Interest Rates. Low interest rates encourage investors to borrow the money needed for development. The money is often created (as if printed) by the central bank, and inflation results. Many policymakers have considered the inflation a "small cost" compared to the benefits of the development projects. The ensuing rise in prices has been the mechanism by which resources have been transferred from those people who (it has often been believed) would otherwise consume them into the hands of investors. The fact that the investors have been mostly rich, and those who paid the higher prices were mostly poor, has not disturbed the policymakers. We have already seen that sometimes the investors have been multinational corporations.

Tariff Policy. This policy includes heavy protection for consumer goods, moderate protection for intermediate goods (and supplies), and low or no protection for machinery imports. The result has been first, the production of goods primarily consumed by the rich (such as automobiles and household appliances); second, discrimination against capital-goods production within LDCs; and third, discrimination against all goods normally produced at home and exports. The first and second of these results are obvious. The third occurs because any tax incentives (such as tariffs) that divert resources to one type of production make those resources scarcer, and hence more expensive, for other types of production. As labor and capital are diverted into ISI consumption goods, they become less available for goods produced by and for the poor. Those goods and LDC exports both tend to be labor intensive. Therefore, the tariff system has promoted unemployment. Since consumer imports are the very goods produced in capital-intensive factories in MDCs, the system has promoted similar factories in LDCs, hence technological dualism.

Investment Incentives. Many LDC governments have offered tax holidays, accelerated depreciation, and other incentives for investment. This in-vestment-incentive policy has reinforced the preceding ones in biasing the production structure toward capital-intensive, modern plants that provide less employment.

High Wages in Modern Enterprises. We have seen (in our discussion of MNCs) how labor unions have forced wages for labor employed in the modern plants to rise much higher than the alternative earning power of labor employed in the urban bazaar or in rural artisanry or farming. Researchers (e.g., Nelson, Schultz, and Slighton 1971) have discovered that in some countries, wages were five or ten times higher in moderen industry than in traditional activities—an example of eco-nomic dualism. Unionism has long been attractive to people who wish to help the poor in industrialized countries, for in those countries, labor organizations have helped to shift incomes from rich to poor. But in LDCs—where union wages rise much more than productivity of labor does—labor unions may instead cause a diversion of income to a small, elite corps of laborers at the expense of unemployment for others. High wages also encourage enterprises (whether government or privately owned) to use less costly machines instead of labor. Such substitution may be appropriate in MDCs, where capital is relatively abundant and labor scarce, but it creates unemployment in LDCs, where labor is readily available and capital expensive.

Exchange Restrictions. Inflation in LDCs has often led to balance-of-payments difficulties. To solve these, LDC governments have imposed restrictions on the purchase of foreign exchange for imports or for travel. In order to keep these restrictions from discouraging ISI, capital imports are frequently exempt, or else licenses are more freely granted for them. Consequently, capital-intensive production (by the rich) is further encouraged, along with technological dualism.

How does indirect government intervention (for ISI) intersect with NIEO? We have already seen that LDC governments have requested preferential access to the markets of MDCs, because without it, the LDCs fear that their share of the manufactured exports of the world would decline. At the same time, ISI has made the price of LDC manufactured goods high, by comparison with world markets, because the LDCs have not produced goods for which they have a natural (comparative) advantage. If LDCs would stress expansion of exports of labor-intensive commodities (as Taiwan, both Koreas, Hong Kong, and Singapore have done), they would most likely be able to bargain their way into the markets of MDCs, and thus not need a GSP. We have also already seen that the manufactured exports of Latin American countries have lagged (proportionately) behind those of NICs. An important reason may be that the Latin American governments are the principal architects of ISI, whereas the East Asian countries (the major NICs) have abandoned it in favor of export promotion.

What finally happens to countries that enact the ISI policy package? Their imports increase rather than decrease, they import more capital goods, and the modern sector spawns rich industrialists and laborers who demand more consumption goods from abroad and more travel. But increased exports are needed to pay for the heavy imports, and the world market for primary products is limited (as we have seen), so the new exports must be manufactured goods. But inefficient, ISI-type manufactures are priced too high for the world market. Hence, ISI countries must depreciate their currencies to balance their international payments. Depreciated currencies mean higher prices at home, and higher prices affect the poor the most.

ISI policies have been criticized by many authors. A number of research papers on ISI that have been written by scholars in the Center for Development Economics at Williams College point to the policies we have mentioned above, but those scholars (e.g., Bruton 1969) carefully say that they are not against *all* ISI, for some imported products can be readily produced at home. The International Labor Organization has done a number of studies on employment in LDCs, and its reports place heavy responsibility upon ISI for aggravating unemployment. Ranis (1973 and 1974), who directed the ILO mission to the Philippines and who has studied the liberalized system of the Taiwanese, is also a principal critic of ISI. In studies sponsored by the National Bureau of Economic Research, Bhagwati (1978) and Krueger (1978) have concluded that distortions introduced by import substitution slowed economic growth in LDCs. All of these critics would agree that ISI may be an appropriate strategy for early development, but that it is usually maintained too long.

Conclusion

In three areas (agriculture and direct and indirect government intervention), we have found that although the internal gaps in LDCs superficially resemble the international gaps, their structures are in fact quite different. NIEO is an appeal both for greater LDC government control over LDC economies, and for transfers of more resources to the LDC elites. The internal gaps, on the other hand, are perpetuated by the kinds of controls LDC governments already are able to exercise, and the internal gaps are associated with transfers from poor to rich. The NIEO plan, coupled with present internal policies, is in large part a program for flows from both ends (foreigners and the poor within LDCs) to the LDC power elites in the middle.

Notes

1. Except for oil and occasional commodity agreements (see Chapter 2).

Bibliography

Barton, Clifton. "Problems and Prospects of Small Industries in the Republic of Vietnam." Saigon: Industrial Development Bank of Saigon, December 1974.
Bauer, P. T. "The Operation and Consequences of the State Export Monopolies of West Africa." In Bauer, P. T., *Dissent on Development: Studies and Debates in Development Economics*, pp. 369–386. Cambridge, Mass.: Harvard University Press, 1972.
———. "The Problem with Foreign Aid." *Wall Street Journal*, June 9, 1980, p. 24.
Bhagwati, J. N. *Anatomy and Consequences of Exchange Control Regimes*. Cambridge, Mass.: Ballinger Publishing Co. for National Bureau of Economic Research, 1978.
Bruton, Henry J. "The Import Substitution Strategy of Economic Development:

A Survey of Findings." Williams College Research Memorandum, no. 27. Unpublished. Williamstown, Mass., 1969.

International Labor Organization. *Matching Employment Opportunities and Expectations: A Programme of Action for Ceylon (Sri Lanka)*. Geneva, 1971.

———. *Employment, Incomes, and Equality: A Strategy for Increasing Productive Employment in Kenya*. Geneva, 1972.

———. *Employment and Income Policies for Iran*. Geneva, 1973.

———. *Sharing in Development: A Programme of Employment, Equity, and Growth for the Philippines*. Geneva, 1974.

———. *Towards Full Employment: A Programme for Colombia*. Geneva, 1974.

Krueger, A. O. *Foreign Trade Regimes and Economic Development: Liberalization Attempts and Consequences*. Cambridge, Mass.: Ballinger Publishing Co. for National Bureau of Economic Research, 1978.

Lewis, Arthur. *The Theory of Economic Growth*. Homewood, Ill.: Irwin, 1955.

Loehr, William, and Powelson, John P. *The Economics of Development and Distribution*. New York: Harcourt, Brace, Jovanovich, 1981.

Nelson, Richard R.; Schultz, T. Paul; and Slighton, Robert L. *Structural Change in a Developing Economy: Colombia's Problems and Prospects*. Princeton, N.J.: Princeton University Press, 1971.

Owen, Wyn F. "The Developmental Squeeze on Agriculture." *American Economic Review* 61:1 (March 1966), 43–70.

Ranis, Gustav. "Industrial Sector Labor Absorption." *Economic Development and Cultural Change* 21:3 (April 1973), 387–408.

———. "Employment, Equity, and Growth: Lessons from the Philippine Employment Mission." *International Labor Review* 110:4 (July 1974), 17–28.

Abbreviations

ECLA	Economic Commission for Latin America
EEC	European Economic Community
GATT	General Agreement on Tariffs and Trade
GDI	gross domestic investment
GDP	gross domestic product
GNP	gross national product
GSP	Generalized System of Preferences
ICOR	incremental capital-output ratio
IDA	International Development Association
ILO	International Labor Organization
IMF	International Monetary Fund
IMS	international monetary system
ISI	import substitution industrialization
LDCs	less developed countries
LDLDCs	least developed countries
MDCs	more developed countries
MFN	most favored nation
MNCs	multinational corporations
NICs	newly industrializing countries
NIEO	New International Economic Order
NOPECs	non-oil-exporting LDCs
NTBs	nontariff barriers
OECD	Organization of Economic Cooperation and Development
OPEC	Organization of Petroleum Exporting Countries

SDRs	Special Drawing Rights
UNCTAD	United Nations Conference on Trade and Development
UNIDO	United Nations Industrial Development Organization
UNITAR	United Nations Institute for Training and Research

Index